From Monks to Mountain Gorillas

Advance praise for *From Monks to Mountain Gorillas*

"*From Monks to Mountain Gorillas* takes the reader on the spiritual journey of the Kaufman family, reconstructing and reconsidering itself in the context of the wider world and the consequences of each member's own actions. Launched by poignant regret of roads not taken and fueled by a passionate desire to explore the universe, Ed Kaufman carries us on an exotic and enlightening pilgrimage of self-discovery."
—STEVE HELLER, author of *What We Choose to Remember*
Professor & Chair, MFA in Creative Writing Program, Antioch University, Los Angeles

"Like the packed flipsides of large format postcards, Kaufman's unpretentious prose will lull you into dangers men half his age wouldn't trade the recliner for. Friend of the world, this not-so-accidental tourist dives into globe trots with a new wife who, as the circumstances demand, calmly sleeps with hyenas or shows her breasts to Ethiopian tribeswomen, and his fearless new son who eats crocodile, calls in elephants and dances with Thai girls who know the "F" word. *From Monks to Mountain Gorillas* will have you wishing you were dancing the twist in Papua New Guinea."
—WAYNE K. SHELDRAKE, author of *Instant Karma: The Heart and Soul of a Ski Bum*

"Kaufman's book bounces readers across the globe to coveted adventure travel sites. Between trips with his intrepid second family, he shares glimpses of their emotional development and family dramas, including his own reckoning with the inevitable."
—DEIRDRE SINNOTT, writer, author, and literary critic

"An exciting read about travels in unexpected places. Dr. Kaufman takes you into the heart of the culture in Tibet, Africa, Borneo and other out-of-the-way places … always with the personal stories that have affected their family. The amazing ability of their son, Adam, to connect with people from entirely different cultures is both humorous and touching. Ed's wife, Karen, is shown as an adventurous woman able to overcome personal and physical trauma to make these travel stories come alive for everyone who reads the book. She is a brilliant photographer. It is with pleasure that I recommend this book to those who love to travel and move away from a comfort zone."
—JANET S. SIMCIC, author of *The Man at the Caffe Farnese* and *An American Chick's Guide to Italy*

"*From Monks to Mountain Gorillas* takes readers to adventure travel destinations with the author, his wife, and young son. Seeking peak experiences without the danger once involved with such experiences, this suburban California family rafts the Colorado, gets close to mega fauna in Tanzania, and mingles with the locals in Papua New Guinea, Namibia, and Indonesia, among other locales. Against this exotic backdrop, ordinary life goes on as Kaufman's son grows up and his own mortality approaches."
—TOBY SULLIVAN, fisherman, poet, journalist, and teacher of creative writing

From Monks to Mountain Gorillas

A Family's Global Adventure

Ed Kaufman

Forked Road Press

Copyright 2011 © Ed Kaufman

ISBN 978-0-9801165-3-3

All rights reserved. No part of this book may be reproduced or transmitted in any form or by any means, electronic or mechanical, including photocopying, recording by an information recording and retrieval system, without express written permission from the publisher.

Forked Road Press
2373 N. Flower St.
Santa Ana, CA 92706
www.forkedroadpress.com

Manufactured in the United States of America.

Cover design: Stephanie Starr

African designs courtesy of Dover Inc.

To my grandsons: Senya Jacob Rogers-Kaufman and Austin Kaufman, my future grandchildren, and their own inner and outer journeys.

"We had achieved in Morocco, maximum family compression, and could only henceforth disperse. Growing up. Leaving home, watching your parents divorce—all in the decade since, have happened. But on a radiant high platform of the Eiffel Tower I felt us still molded, it seemed, forever together."
—JOHN UPDIKE, *My Father's Tears*

Contents

Introduction
1. Two Green Chairs • *1*
2. Passages Through the Grand Canyon • *7*
3. Mongo: Adventures in a Country Home • *21*
4. Pillow Wrestling • *29*
5. A Cautious Family's First African Adventure • 33
6. Back to Africa • *43*
7. A Home by the Sea • 63
8. Feh! • 67
9. Wedding in Saraburi • 71
10. After the Tsunami • 79
11. The Blind Leading the Blind • 83
12. How Adam Coped with a Tibetan Trip at Ten • *91*
13. Tibetan Brotherhood • *111*
14. On Our Own in Alaska • *115*
15. Stirring in Sayulita • *127*

16. Eddie Spaghetti • *131*
17. Sex in the Galapagos • *135*
18. Survival in the Galapagos • *139*
19. Catalina Island • *151*
20. Himba Happiness • *159*
21. Papua Pride • *163*
22. To Live and Die in Varanasi • *171*
23. Mercy Mursi • *175*
24. Touched by a Gorilla • *181*
25. Lalibella Liturgy • *185*
26. Sundays with Senya • *189*
27. My Thai Grandson • *193*
28. When Karen Fell Off Her Ass on Her Ass • *197*
29. From Purgatory to Puya • *201*
30. Burning Man • *205*
31. Fiftieth Medical School Reunion • *209*
32. An Independent Surfer • *213*
33. Ed's Epiphany • *217*

Acknowledgements

Locations for each chapter

Introduction

After their second safari to Africa, contemplating what each member of his family had gained, Ed Kaufman writes:

"Adam had [. . .] remained calm in the presence of lions, and not backed down from a troop of baboons. He had survived two weeks without peers and not shed a tear. Karen had looked a hyena in the eye, stood ten feet from rhinos, and befriended a medicine woman. She had learned that it was worth braving latrines and cold showers if adventures awaited her. I had survived being thrown about like a rag doll by the turbulent waters of the Zambezi despite a warning from my deceased father. All three of us had sat toe to trunk with a herd of elephants and not flinched [. . .]."

Under the surface of every adventure chronicled in this book lies the substratum of themes about freedom and courage, freedom from conforming to the ways of America, the courage to confront the edges where fear lives, fortified by the sheer exhilaration of extraordinary adventures.

In the opening adventures, we see Adam spotting a safari's first lion, "a flash of tawny pelt moving between the wheat-hued grasses." We see Karen on a trip down the Colorado River glide to the front of "the bouncy, air-filled rubber pontoon," whooping and hollering with delight, Ed grasping Adam by the life jacket as the pontoon boat "is hit by an inexpugnable wall as hundreds of gallons of water" pour over them, before they "plunge into a flume of fat air."

Imperceptibly, later on, the adventures change, expand. Ed's oldest son Alex gets married in a Buddhist Temple in Thailand where he lives; sixteen months later, when they visit again, they are in the Thailand destroyed by a tsunami. In a father-son expedition to a remote bay in Kodiak Island, Alaska, to visit a writing colleague, Ed and Adam fly on a four-seater floatplane, fish for halibut from a skiff, and sample the professional side of salmon fishing. In Zimbabwe, while Karen, Ed, and Adam are relaxing beside a pool, a herd of elephants, trunks only inches away from their feet, come to drink. In Costa Rica, "the grunting chants of howler monkeys" awakens them just before they kayak solo into a windstorm.

Ed's descriptions are so thrilling they put us right there in the moment. His insights into the family's reactions as they master the challenges of progressively more extreme travel chronicle the human side of these intoxicating journeys.

These are extraordinary adventures undertaken by ordinary people, one family's journey from the near to the far realms of exotic travel. These are also the author's journeys into a challenge of equal if not greater dimension, the pursuit of the art and craft of writing creative nonfiction. In the spirit of the adventure writers like Redmond O'Hanlon, travel writers like Jonathan Raban, humorous writers like Bill Bryson, though in a voice uniquely his own, Ed guides the reader through transformative journeys of psychic and family life. In this venture too, in these compressed to the marrow pieces, his accomplishments soar into some breathtaking passages.

In the most touching moments of the book, Ed probes his own quest: questions about death and mortality, spirituality and belief. Here, in these passages, when the author records his own truth, a raw honesty emerges that shines a different kind of luminosity on all the adventures. Here at last we come to see the driving thirst to break through the boundaries of material understanding and move toward self-knowledge that is the center of this book and this writer, the restless unwillingness to settle for quotidian answers that propels him, even late in life's arc, into exotic and sometimes dangerous travel and new realms of achievement. The link between spirituality and writing, lurking in the subtext, becomes visible here, showing itself in the gleaming moments when adventure and significance unite.

—JULIE BRICKMAN
Laguna Beach, 2011
What Birds Can Only Whisper
Fiction Faculty, Spalding University
MFA in Writing Program

1

Two Green Chairs

Philadelphia, May 1960

When I was mid-way through medical school, my mother was given two tufted, green leatherette chairs with gold buttons. She said, "These chairs are for your waiting room when you practice medicine—in our home."

The chairs were finer than any we had in our house and we placed them by the front window where I tried to relax and read.

I lived at home through college and medical school, moving from one row house Philadelphia neighborhood to another, whenever a family of color moved in nearby. My father said we had to act quickly before property values dropped. I tried to move away from home several times but always backed down when Mom's arthritis caused her a great deal of pain or when she accused me, with good reason, of wanting to sleep with "those sexy nurses."

My intention was to marry a few days after graduation from medical school, two events that should have helped me leave home. Still, my mother needed me to intern close by and couldn't stand the idea of my leaving to live with my new wife. Mom found her too tall, too thin, too nervous, and too much of a hippy. Besides, no one was perfect enough for her Eddie.

I confided in a favorite professor that my mother was acting as if it would devastate her if I were to move.

"I know I need to leave," I said, "but I don't want to hurt her. What can I do?"

"I struggled when my sons left," he replied. "I knew they had to go away to school. One even went to Canada. They had to separate. So do you."

The results of the intern match arrived on a balmy spring day. My first choices were two local hospitals I knew wouldn't accept me. I blamed a computerized program for the assignment to Los Angeles County General, as far away as I could get.

Dad stood in the background, scowled and said, "If you go there it will kill your mother." My seventeen-year-old sister, about to attend a local nursing school, cowered in a remote corner. Mom saw through my subterfuge and trembled. I watched her reflection in the worn gilded mirror as she pounded her arthritically gnarled fists.

"Go! Just go!" she shrieked. She paused for a moment, then whimpered, "You can't have those chairs for your waiting room now!"

"Save them for me, Mom. I'll be back in a year."

"I don't care if you ever come back!" she shouted.

I did come back east to New York, not Philly, a year later for my psychiatry residency. I visited my mother, though not often. When I did, I sat in my inescapable chair, unable to leave the house to visit my friends. I set up my first practice in New York, and moved the green chairs, by now a bit tattered, to the office where I sat with my patients. A few years later, Mom took a rare trip to New York City. Her tour left no time to visit, but she asked if she could call.

"No, Mother. I'll be with my patients." I droned in my psychiatric voice.

She importuned, "What would be so bad if you just said, 'Hello, Mom,' in front of your patient?"

I explained to her about professional anonymity, but she couldn't accept the concept, particularly if it meant we couldn't speak when she was visiting my city.

A year later she was stricken with rapidly progressive gall bladder cancer, her immunity weakened by years of steroids for arthritis. My father stopped me before I entered her hospital room.

"We can't tell your mother she has cancer. It's just too depressing for her to hear that dreaded word. She thinks she has a gallstone." The word cancer was unspeakable then. We did not have a medical term as frightening until AIDS struck twenty years later.

Mom was surrounded by her siblings and tended to by my sister, dressed in a nursing uniform she hadn't worn in years because she had left the profession to become an academic researcher. I hoped mother didn't see my shock when I first caught sight of her cancer-ridden body. After everyone else left the room, I tried to figure out if she were willing to talk about her illness because it was important to me that we finally have a dialogue not based on denial.

"Mom, I hear the Doc has you on antidepressants."

"Yeah, I just cry all the time and I don't eat."

"Weight loss can be caused by depression, but I don't think that's the reason now."

"I'm losing weight because of the nausea caused by the gall stone."

She wasn't ready to tell me she knew, if indeed she did know, that she was suffering from an incurable disease. She died a few months later at fifty-three, acting all the while as if she didn't know she was dying.

After her death, I struggled back to full-time practice. I often stared at the chairs and regretted that I hadn't spoken to her the day she came to New York, even that I hadn't sat with her one last time. I hunkered into one of the chairs and saw my mom in the other, as she was when I was seven, before her joints became swollen and misshapen—when she taught me to love books and could still paint pictures that I proudly took to school every holiday. Yet the memory of her shriveled yellowed body lying in that bed pretending she didn't have cancer replaced the vibrant image of her youth.

The following year I submitted my research for publication for the first time. I completed psychoanalytic training and accepted a coveted academic position. The time had arrived. I replaced the green leatherette seats with a teak and black leather analytic couch and matching office chairs. The new furniture was sleek and modern, without gold buttons.

Forty years later, I still regret that we didn't sit together the last time she visited New York. I missed my chance to tell her about my life as a father of my own children and the world I was beginning to explore. My adventure travels would have scared her half to death, and if she were alive I might not have been able to go on many of them. Today, I invite her and my readers to sit with me in two elegant green chairs and listen to the family adventures that I experienced after her death.

2

Passages Through the Grand Canyon

Colorado, Summer 2003

Karen cautiously moves up from her safe seat on the ice chest at the back of the raft to the front of the bouncy, air-filled rubber pontoon.

It is the last full day of our family's Colorado River trip through the Grand Canyon. The trip was once so frightening to Karen that the night before we were to leave, she begged Adam, now nine, and me, to not go. Now she is sitting on the front of the pontoons, the most dangerous and exhilarating spot on the boat. We are approaching Lava, a Class 10 rapid with a drop of thirteen feet.

It has been two hours since we left our lunch site at Havasu Creek. Karen, riding the perilous pontoon through three moderate rapids, whoops and hollers with delight. We pass Vulcan's Anvil, a large volcanic rock jutting out of the water, which means that we are only one mile from Lava. Bruce, our guide, shouts "Down and in!" The eleven passengers all hop off the pontoons and crouch on the bottom of the boat. We hold fast to the ropes on either side of us. My left hand grasps Adam tightly by his life jacket while I dig my right foot hard and fast into the crease of the pontoon. A 20-foot wall of water comes at us like a tidal wave. The boat dips down into the wave and is hit by an inexpungable liquid wall as hundreds of gallons of water pour over us. We plunge into a flume of fat air and when I open my eyes I gape into a huge black hole formed by Lava's double wave. Everyone on the boat is screaming, but I can't make out a word.

I have just enough time to take a deep breath before we are struck by a tsunami-like burst of water. Adam screams, "We're going to die." In a minute, which feels like an eternity, we pass through safely and Adam cries out, "So cool, soooo cool!"

Karen shrieks, "It is fantastic."

I grin smugly, which means I knew she'd love it if she let herself go. We breathe a sigh of relief as we jump back on top of the pontoons and are hit by the second ridge of Lava. This part of the rapid has only half the slam-intensity, so Adam, Karen, and I are able to keep our eyes open throughout the full impact of its strike. We enjoy being rocked through the wavy froth as we watch the waves roll over and around us.

Karen and I have hiked the Grand Canyon many times. We've wanted to raft the Colorado ever since the first time cool contented rafters waved to us when we made our way down the hot canyon to the welcome respite of the river on a sticky summer day. We researched the possibility of navigating the river with Adam and were assured it was perfectly safe to take him on a five-day motorized pontoon boat trip.

In August of Adam's ninth summer, Karen, Adam, and I drove from our home in Laguna Beach, California, to Marble Canyon, Arizona, to start our 182-mile raft trip. We arrived in plenty of time for the orientation meeting, which was held in a cramped room at the side of a rustic gas station. Most of the tour group had their flights delayed by lightning storms and were irritable, grumpy, and preoccupied with the discomfort and fear they had experienced on their turbulent trip. Adam, always sociable, told the hassled travelers about the fires he saw on our way and the thundershowers that evaporated before the water hit the ground. They looked through him without a response. I hoped they wouldn't stay this crabby for the rest of the trip.

The restaurant at the launch point displayed large photographs of boats capsizing and smashing into rocks with wood splintering in every direction and passengers flying through the air. Books for sale had titles like *Death on the Colorado*. Karen looked at the photos and her shoulders shrank in a resolute shrug, meaning she may not come along with us.

She wagged her finger and said, "Did you see those boats smashing on the river we're planning to raft tomorrow?"

Although formerly a competitive swimmer in high school, Karen avoids choppy water because she is sensitive to motion sickness, another reason not to go on the river.

Our boatman, Bruce, increased her fears by telling Karen that he'd only rafted the Colorado three times. Karen, usually quite aware, was unable to take in his teasing grin; her fear had paralyzed her perceptions. Bruce, tall, tan, and angular, introduced us to his assistant, Quentin, an experienced boatman who was quite new to this part of the river, another fact that caused Karen to quiver. Quentin was chubby for a river guide and had a full, scruffy beard. He was the company's main guide on the upper Colorado through Cataract Canyon, a trip we would take with him as our guide the following year.

Bruce announced, "There are no portable showers on this trip. The Colorado River temperature is 45 degrees Fahrenheit, and the air will reach at least 115 degrees."

Karen, now annoyed as well as frightened, whispered, "Five days of heat, dirt, and port-a-potties. My idea of a vacation is a peaceful state of mind. You and Adam go, and I'll meet you back here in five days—or maybe none of us should go." Adam and I looked at each other and exchanged a glance that conveyed we knew Karen meant business. There was a good chance the trip might not take place for us unless we could be very persuasive.

"Mom, we need you," he pleaded. "We've planned this for a year,"

Raising my voice, I begged her to reconsider. "Karen, you wanted to cancel the Inca Trail the night before and it was one of our greatest life experiences. This will be too."

Karen's brow furrowed, reflecting images of boats splintering on rocks and the critical admonitions of her friends, but she hesitatingly agreed to go with the unspoken acknowledgment that if anything went wrong, it would be "Ed's fault."

The next morning we were in our life jackets and on our pontoon boats by 8:30 in order to start our trip from Lee's Ferry. The boatmen skillfully loaded the boat and lowered it into the chilly water. The canyon wall, made of three types of stone, is only 470 feet high at this point.

Bruce had guided over eighty trips down the Colorado River, and recently returned from kayaking it from one end to the other. He knew every turn and pebble. Karen's brow finally softened.

As we passed under the Navajo Bridge at mile five, an attractive young woman waved to us and dropped a capsule that Bruce retrieved. He read the note inside and a mischievous smile broadened his face.

No more than 150 people a day are permitted to leave Lee's Ferry. Our boat was the only motor-powered one that left that day, so we rapidly outdistanced the others. We chose the motorized pontoon because the minimum age is eight in contrast to age twelve requirements for oar-powered trips. The substantial size and cushiony pontoons provide amazing comfort and help the boat take the waves with power and balance. The Colorado has its own ratings system from 1 to 10, in contrast to the usual I to V International Whitewater Scale. In either system, waves are rated by the skill required to navigate them as well as their size and degree of danger. Bruce told us that we would attempt several 10s.

Our family rapidly became aware of the paradoxical nature of the Colorado River as it traversed the Grand Canyon. Most of the time, the Colorado was peaceful, docile and rhythmically meditative, as we drifted with the three or four-mile-per-hour downstream current or powered the boat up to ten miles per hour. We slowed down to the rhythm of the river. On the other hand, riding rapids rated 3 or 4 out of 10 is invigorating and riding a 10, like Lava Falls, is as exciting as anything most people have ever done in their lives. The only man-made experience that comes close for me is the upside down part of the loop-the-loop on a roller coaster.

The walls of the canyons rapidly climbed above us and enveloped us with an ever-changing, uncluttered view of shades of brown, black, gray, red, and green. New layers emerged every day, and we were able to count thirty by the end of our trip where the Canyon was a mile deep and recapitulated the formation of the crusts of the earth. The quiet walls emitted the peace of the 1.8 billion years of age of their oldest layer. Nature has carved a myriad of ancient faces into the walls of the canyon. Adam saw many faces in the rocks and Karen remarked, "You can experience the feelings of the lost souls that are trapped inside."

Because the nights were so warm that tents would be stifling, we slept under the stars and on top of our sleeping bags, placed on metal cots assembled by each family. I don't know why it should be so difficult to put together a simple cot, but it was for me, at least the first few times. I kept confusing left with right and up with down. The portable toilet was called a groover, since it left grooves on the user's thighs or maybe because it was always placed in groovy places with great views of the Colorado River.

We hiked a quarter of a mile to a point just above a small rapid. Karen, Adam, and I shifted our life vests to our bottoms and fastened them like diapers, enabling us to slide down the rapids about 500 feet. We slid feet first on our backs and were able to steer by moving our legs and butts and wiggling our shoulders. Karen and I giggled downstream, reminiscing about sliding into swimming pools as children.

Another half-mile hike took us to a 15-foot-high rock, which overlooked a swimming hole. By the time Karen and I arrived, we heard Adam screaming with joy as he jumped for the second time. Karen shrieked his name, but she could see that he was already an expert. Hesitatingly, I leaped in, the first time I have ever jumped from such a height into water. Karen joined me, and when we surfaced, we turned around and looked at the panorama of nature that surrounded us. There were waterfalls tumbling and roaring from every angle and just beyond them, the multi-colored and majestic canyon walls. After Adam jumped off the rocks several more times, we hiked back to our original water rapids slide. We put our life jackets back on our behinds, and the current took us the full quarter mile back to the boat.

By the end of our second day, the canyon wall was 3,800 feet high. The limestone layer contained fossils of 400-million-year-old fish, ferns and insects. In the upper layers of sandstone were 250-million-year-old dinosaur tracks.

Our second campsite was 65 miles from our starting point. We settled in at a flat, sandy beach with a panoramic view of the river and falls and ate freshly barbecued chicken. Adam and I fished for rainbow trout. He loves to fish and I enjoy teaching him what little I know about fishing. I helped him bait his hook and cast without tangling his line. I showed him how to put his finger on the line, to sense when a fish is nibbling on the bait, jerk the line, set the hook and reel the fish in. Adam's dimples flashed in a joyous smile when he caught the trout, worked it off the hook, returned it to the river and watched it swim away.

Karen was perfectly relaxed by now, and her workday stresses and pre-trip fears had dissipated. "It's so soothing to be taken care of," she said, "to have all your meals prepared and served, not to have to cook or clean and not to be hassled by anything; not household, school, Adam's piano practice or his homework. I love the solitude, the peacefulness of the river, the excitement of the rapids and passing through almost two billion years of the earth's history. What could be better?"

Quentin told stories of previous river trips he'd led on the upper Colorado. His favorite tales were of Italian tourists who made the entire trip in alligator shoes, linen pants and silk shirts, and Boy Scouts who ate so much food that with two days left the only remaining provisions were peanut butter and jelly without bread. He recalled several wives who were duped by their husbands into believing there were luxury lodges along the river. One of these women dealt with her anger by sipping vodka from morning till night, until Quentin had to take it away from her. Then she complained so bitterly, he gave it back. He spoke of his love of photography and literature. "When I retire I want to become an English teacher," he told me. I thought about how many of my friends would like to do the opposite, quit teaching and spend their lives in national parks.

We left our campsite before 8 a.m. in order to traverse twenty-three rapids, some with drops of 30 feet. At mile 76, a jet-black layer of Vishnu Schist emerged at the base of the canyon. The schist contains fossils of one-celled animals, the beginning of life on our planet. Two miles downriver, we rode the 19-foot drop of Sockdolager, which means "knockout punch." Just after Zoroaster Rapid, we passed under the suspension bridges of the Kaibab and Bright Angel trails and waved joyously to hikers as they approached the river. Karen and I rode on top of the pontoons through Granite, which is Class 7-8. We suddenly descended 18 feet and huge waves hit us from both sides. A monster wave bounced off the canyon wall and knocked me off the front right pontoon, but fortunately toward the inside of the boat.

Another mile downriver we reached Hermit, rated "only" a 7-8, but one of my favorite rapids. Hermit is made up of five spectacular waves. The fifth and largest swell grabbed the raft and held it captive at a dangerous angle before it let us pass safely through. We were "down and in" for Hermit, which means we squatted on the floor with our heads tucked in. Three more miles brought us to Crystal Rapid, which can rate 10-plus. We handled Crystal easily by staying to the extreme right and avoiding a whirlpool that could have sucked us into the jagged boulders known as the "Rock Garden" down below. Later in the afternoon we stopped at Shinumo Falls where the water was again warm and clear. I let the soothing waters wash over me as I basked in the beauty of the majestic waterfall formed by

Shinumo Creek.

We left early on day four to stop at Royal Arch Creek by a waterfall framed by fern and moss-covered boulders. We were able to climb up the moist hollow behind the falls to a rock window overlooking the water's cascade. Everyone jumped through the slippery portal into the pool below. I was the last to try it, again overcoming my fears of leaping off rocks into water and letting myself go.

By now, Karen had learned to enjoy the rapids as much as the stillness. We no longer used our watches as we were on Canyon Time. We ate our meals and set our goals for the day only by the position of the sun. It was the best antidote for long, busy workdays. At first Adam repeatedly asked the time, until Bruce taught Adam to look up at the sun and know when it was time to eat or camp. We ate lunch that day by Stone Creek Waterfall, where we splashed through the warm stream that led to Deer Creek Falls.

The walls of the canyon now climbed to 5,000 feet above us. Karen looked up at the canyon's layers at mile 135 and realized that she had grown more courageous as the sheets of rock were revealed.

On day five the group made an early departure in order to maximize time at Havasu Creek. There are hundreds of magnificent pools created by the creek as it makes its way seven miles to the Colorado. We hiked up the creek trail for about a mile until we came to a complex of six pools formed by tall rocks where we jumped into pools of clear, warm water. Our crew played joyfully, jumping and tossing Adam like a beach ball, and swimming for a leisurely two hours. After our hike back, we ate a lunch of chicken salad, cheese, tomatoes, onions, and pastrami. We crowded under a medium-sized beach umbrella to eat our lunch semi-protected from the boiling hot sun, and then returned to the boat, ready to take on Lava Falls.

One mile before reaching Lava we saw Vulcan's Anvil, a towering deposit of basalt in the middle of the river. It was formed over a million years ago when a volcano erupted and spewed lava over 74 miles of the Colorado River. The lava dammed the river and caused a huge lake behind it, but this has gradually eroded away, leaving only Vulcan's Anvil as a visible reminder.

Lava Falls was a Grand Canyon legend feared even by the river guides. Its bubbling turbulence extended from one side of the river to the other, a 10 at any water level. With the skill of our guides, we challenged and conquered the chasm of its deep V-shaped wave.

Bruce said it was 120 degrees that day and it was still stifling at night. Adam, Karen, and I camped in a shady site by the river so close to the water that my cot practically fell in, but we were cooler at the river's edge.

The last morning, we rode our boat five miles to the helicopter pad, which was 182 miles from the start of our journey. The helicopter swooped down and cut in against the cliff, taking the three of us up to a ranch where a plane waited to take us back to Marble Canyon. Scaling the walls of the canyon, we were enveloped by two billion years of earth's history. I said to Adam, "Half of our planet's past is in these walls."

His answer: "Dad, the walls are even older than you."

Karen sang, "Take me to the river," a refrain she would repeat many times in the months that followed.

3

MONGO:
ADVENTURES IN A COUNTRY HOME
Long Island, Summer 1976

SUMMERS IN SHELTER ISLAND, New York, in the mid-1970s were a journey back in time to a haven where fish were abundant, fragrant lilacs bloomed, Victorian houses flourished unrestored, and scallops clacked on shore by the ton. *Blazing Saddles* played in a nearby theater and my sons and I roared at its raunchy humor.

My sons from my first family—Alex, eleven at the time, and Tony, four—were both at ages where they could appreciate movies with strong farting scenes, and this movie had one of the best. In the film, corrupt government officials meet with a group of criminals around a campfire where they eat baked beans and plan to take over a town. The boys and I broke up laughing as the cowboys ate more and more baked beans and produced a variety of cacophonic fart sounds. Alex Karras, a former football player, plays a muscular cowhand called Mongo. He is brutishly strong and, at first, seems rather stupid. He knocks out a horse with one blow, sets his hat on fire when he lights his cigar, communicates mainly by grunts and threatening utterances, and has chains crisscrossing his chest in a vain attempt to keep his great physical power in check.

Prior to seeing *Blazing Saddles*, Alex and his friends played a rough and tumble version of hide-and-seek in the woods behind our house. The boys liked the game best when I was it and instead of racing them back to a tree, I tackled them and held them down until they gave up. They eluded me by running through the woods, swinging on vines, and finding hiding places from which to pelt me with crabapples that they stockpiled by the bushel. After seeing the movie, I became my own version of Mongo, shifting to a lurching but menacing walk, my hands curved downwards, elbows bent upwards, uttering guttural, inarticulate sounds (*whehh, ehggg, mongooo*).

Shelter Island in the Watergate era was an oasis from the hectic pace of Manhattan and even from the rapidly populating Hamptons. The island to this day is reachable only by ferry from either fork at the tip of Long Island.

I traveled by train and bus to the North Fork of Long Island on Friday evenings to join my family. As I approached the house, I wondered what Alex and his two

Mongo

local buddies had planned for our weekend Mongo game. They spent hours every week preparing plans of attack and escape. The boys freed vines from the trees to swing into the woods behind our house, fortified their clubhouse on top of the barn with junk taken from the local garbage dump, stored apples and nuts in tree houses, and dug an elaborate network of tunnels.

I asked my wife Ellen what the boys had in mind for our battle that weekend, but she acted as if she had no idea. She disclosed that Tony, dreadfully frightened by previous hostilities, was planning to join us this time. A psychiatric colleague and former Italian Rugby player, Paul, was dropping by and wanted to join Mongo.

"Not that animal!" Ellen cried. "He's too much for the boys."

The rules of Mongo were simple; the boys could do almost anything they wanted, except spit or hit me in the face. When flushed out of their hideout, I tackled and held them down and gave them the choice of giving up or having their ear bitten. They never gave up, so I often nibbled.

While I was reading in the sunroom on a foggy Saturday morning, our next-door neighbors came by and asked with toothless grins and ingratiating smiles when Mongo would begin. Leslie and John were heavily freckled with home bowl-cut hair, flattened faces and tattered jeans overalls. Leslie, though twelve, was built like a bull.

I encouraged Tony to join the older boys and he did

so hesitantly, because Mongo was outlandishly intimidating to him. With Paul coming, I would have a partner for the first time and one who was strong and aggressive, yet playful. This had the possibility of being the greatest Mongo battle of them all and I didn't want Tony to miss it.

Paul arrived on time. My God, he was big! He weighed at least 275 pounds and had menacing sharp features, threatening dark eyes, thick bushy eyebrows and a shaved head. Was it fair to turn this huge rugby player into an assistant Mongo in a struggle against four boys, whose cumulative ages added up to thirty-seven years? What mattered was how much fun we would all have without anyone being hurt. But could someone be hurt this time?

Paul and I walked to the edge of the woods, 100 feet beyond the house and 50 feet past the edge of the barn. There was not a sound anywhere except robins, blue jays, and red-winged blackbirds rustling in the bushes. The woods were thick with heavy gnarled vines hanging from oak and maple trees. Paul and I saw the clearing the boys had made and started tentatively into the opening. John darted through the back of the woods. We raced toward him, but he disappeared. We heard a scurrying behind us and sensed that the boys had changed positions, and then we saw John scoot toward the spot where the sounds were coming from, so we cut him off. Paul kept watch while I chased John. He dodged left and right but was not as strong as the others. Once I placed my hands on him, I subdued him easily. He hated having his ear munched and was already crying when I wrestled him to the ground. "You fat bastard," he shouted, hurling his spit in my face as I gave him the option of giving up.

"You broke the rules, John." I shouted. I took the top of his ear in my mouth and let him go with no physical damage but with a great blow to his pride. He pleaded to be permitted to join the other boys, and I agreed, rejoining Paul.

Paul and I sat and talked about the strains in our marriages, if and when we would divorce, and waited. We estimated the boys would come out as soon as it was close to lunchtime. No sign of them, after an endless hour, not even Tony, who should have been starving by now. Paul and I gave up waiting and started to tramp into the clearing in the woods. We saw an area of loose dirt and dug until we unearthed a trap door made from an orange crate. We lifted it up and I gave a Mongo grunt into the dark hole. The only reply was a slight whimper, which I recognized as a sound Tony makes when frightened. Paul bellowed, 'Come out now when you have a chance!" No answer. Paul tried to squeeze his body into the opening, but there was no way he could even begin to get his huge frame into the passage. I weighed seventy-five pounds less, but the entrance was also impossible for me to pass through. The dark hole intimidated me and felt like a potential ambush, another reason to stay out.

Paul said, "Let's smoke them out."

I hesitated, "Paul, those are my children and their friends!"

"They won't get hurt, they have a way out."

"Paul, I'm not sure it's safe. It won't take much smoke in those narrow tunnels to suffocate them."

I felt this was kind of crazy, but carried away in the heat of the moment there was no way to turn back.

"OK, Paul, this will be a game none of us will ever forget," I said. We put a few dry leaves and sheets of newspaper in the tunnel and set them on fire. Smoke seeped into the subterranean passages and wisps of it came up from the forest floor.

I panicked and suddenly screamed, "Paul, what are we doing? Tony's in there!"

A moment later, the boys popped their heads out about forty feet away. They had navigated their way through the series of elaborate tunnels they had spent weeks digging. They hopped on swinging vines back to their clubhouse at the top of the barn.

Paul and I charged up the steps, but they locked the door. We shook and banged on it. Paul rocked back, then surged forward with the full weight of his shoulder. The door splintered open and there sat the boys surrounded by their rusty radio parts, broken TVs and old Playboy magazines. Wide-eyed in fear and wondering what Paul and I would do next, they were now defeated. There was no need to bite any ears after the smoke-out and shattered door. The boys were so frightened they surrendered and the battle was over. Paul and I hopped down the stairs as they called out in unison, "Can Paul come back next week?"

Tony was in general, and even more so on the day of the smoke out, frightened by the game of Mongo. This incident was the first and last time he would play. The next summer, Ellen and I sold the house and moved to California in what we later realized was a last attempt to save our marriage.

4

Pillow Wrestling

California 2004

Almost three decades have passed since I last played Mongo. I am now husband and father in my second family. My third son Adam, at age ten, often challenges me to our own version of the contest, a gentler type of wrestling we call Pillow. He has three precious pillows: his favorite, tan with a racing car pattern; another one, blue with dolphins and turtles; and a third, plain white with buttons and a pocket that becomes a mouth. We often use all three in the game. Even at ten, Adam assumes a soothing childish voice when he speaks to Pillow.

To start the game, I wrench the pillows from his hands, but take care not to rip their worn covers. I toss them just out of his reach, hold his body firmly to make it difficult for him to squirm away, and recapture them. I clasp him closely; the feeling of skin to skin, the thumping of my older heart against the thin wall of his chest, the mingling of youthful freshness with the fetid odors of aging, the awareness of his muscles growing and testing me all combine to comprise the ecstatic father-son intimacy of rough-housing.

I wonder if Pillow evolved and persisted because of my age, fifty-eight when Adam was born, the loss of male hormones that goes with aging, or merely the sweet interaction that takes place between us when we wrestle with pillows as the prize. Sometimes I am self-conscious about how much pleasure the intimate contact gives me, but it was Adam's favorite thing we did together just as Mongo was his brother Alex's favorite game.

Our Yellow Labrador, Crystal, joined our family when Adam was five years old. She squirms into the game, scratching us lightly, licking us with her wet, sloppy tongue and squeezing her 72-pound body between us. When Crystal plays, we giggle her name hilariously, but she won't help me by running off with Pillow.

When Adam heard about Mongo he begged to see a video of *Blazing Saddles*. We curled up on the couch together to watch the Mel Brooks classic. Adam loved the farting scene at the campfire even more than his brothers. I explained how I tried to take on the brute strength of Mongo when I battled with Alex and his friends and described the game's details.

"Can we play on the hillside at the back of our house?" Adam asked. I wondered if my body were up for this rough and tumble game and responded, "Maybe in a few weeks."

I often daydream of Tony and Alex coming from their homes in Brooklyn and Thailand and playing with us. Powerful feelings of nostalgia start in my chest and slowly bring tears to my eyes when I think about all three playing this game from so long ago. The four of us have been together so rarely; I wouldn't even care who was on my side. Maybe Tony would be Mongo just this one time.

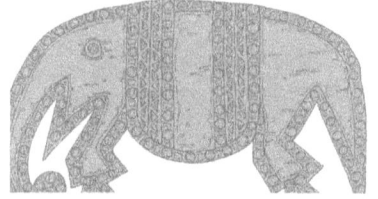

5

A CAUTIOUS FAMILY'S FIRST AFRICAN ADVENTURE

Tanzania, Summer 2001

A HERD OF ZEBRAS SUDDENLY BOLT. My son screams, "A lion! A lion jumped! It's in the brush." Karen and I can't see the lion and suspect it is a product of Adam's wishful seven-year-old imagination. A flash of tawny pelt moves between the wheat-hued grasses. We pull over. Adam and I stand up through the open roof of the Land Rover.

Adam shouts, "I saw a lion. I spotted it." Jack, another seven-year-old in a nearby car, challenges him with "Sure, sure you did, Adam." Suddenly three powerful lionesses move stealthily through the bush. Karen and I barely glimpse them, yet I tremble at my first peek of these magnificent animals. I dreamt for years of seeing lions on the plains of Africa and here they were at last. Adam triumphantly sways his hips from side to side, pumps his fists victoriously in the air. "Yes," he cries out, "oh yes, oh yes!"

This took place in Tarangire National Park in Tanzania, where lion sightings are rare. The pride was the first sighting of a big cat in the wild for any of the eleven tourists on the safari. I was exhilarated by the lions' power and the implied danger of being so close to them, even in the safety of a Land Rover. I feared the lion could jump on top of the Rover and pounce on us. As groundless as the fear was, surviving my fantasy of danger added excitement and triumph.

Safari in Swahili means journey. We had taken a seemingly endless journey to get to this African national park and were anticipating a life-changing experience, even more so after seeing our first lions. We chose family-friendly Thompson Safari as our guides, and our first morning they arranged to have students from the Sakila School dance and sing for us to the beat of a youthful drummer. Adam met his eight-year-old pen pal, Frederick, dressed in blue shorts and a starched white shirt. The Tanzanian children proved to be great soccer players on a rocky field. They let Jack score two goals and tried to let Adam score, but he missed. Jack and his dad exchanged high fives and Adam briefly lost his perpetual smile.

We were treated to a lunch featuring the local starch staple, Ugali, a smooth corn meal mush smothered in meat sauce. Dora, the wife of our guide John, prepared the meal. Karen urged Dora to show her how to put on the traditional Tanzanian skirt and headpiece. Dora and her friends giggled along with Karen as she dressed and undressed in their outfits. John's children rode rickety bikes made entirely of wood. The square wheels worked far better downhill than up. Adam and I were amazed that they worked at all.

The following day we had travelled to Tarangire National Park and from 150 yards away we observed a herd of zebras. I took as many pictures as I could and checked the animals off on a list in an attempt to claim them without killing them. The park was filled with herds of zebras, elephants, giraffes, and gazelles, the giraffes regal and statuesque as they gently ambled from tree to tree. When I watched them through binoculars they turned and looked me right in the eye, charming me with their long eyelashes. By the end of the day I took fewer and fewer pictures. Was I becoming discriminating, jaded, or beginning to leave photography to Karen?

It was at Tarangire where Adam had spotted his first lion with an 'Oh yeah,' giving him a role as assistant guide. After the lions, everything seemed tame until a herd of elephants became suspicious and protective of their babies. They charged our car, flared out their ears, and made threatening bleating sounds. John said in his dead-pan way, "Ellies can and have overturned Land Rovers. We better get out fast." I was relieved when, despite his warnings, he urged us to get pictures of the elephants before they charged.

Our next adventure was a hike with a Maasai warrior. Maasai are tall, thin, and elegant in their bearing. He wore a traditional red plaid blanket and beaded earrings in his elongated earlobes. He carried a long spear; his confident bearing communicated that he could use it if necessary. The first animals we saw on this hike were "toilet seat" waterbucks named for the markings on their backsides. Adam couldn't stop laughing at the name "toilet seat" and his giggling alerted elephants parading nearby, so the guide shushed him. This was our first encounter with elephants outside the protection of our vehicle. Wild elephants are menacing to encounter on foot even with the protection of a guide. Could he stop them if they charged? The Maasai apparently didn't want to find out and warned us to head home before we were attacked.

Adam bragged to the warrior, "I spotted a lion today." He was told, "Lions are afraid of the Maasai. We kill lions!"

Until recent concerns about lion preservation, killing a lion was an adolescent rite of passage for Maasai.

The Hazda And Datoga Tribes

As we neared the Kadero Mountains, we stopped at the villages of two local rural tribes, the Hazda and Datoga. One Datoga woman at first refused to have her picture taken. John explained to her in Swahili we were from America. She whispered to him and he responded with a big laugh, saying she'd asked, "Why do they want my picture? Don't they have Datoga in America?" She gave in, and Karen began her series of photos of tribal men and women with her picture of this frail, toothless, lively woman with hoops stretching her lower earlobes. Karen had no idea at that moment to what extent this type of photography would eventually change her life.

The Hazda men along the road were almost naked. They were Adam's height but muscular. They had broad grins and insisted on shaking our hands, but wouldn't let us take their pictures until we gave them ten cents for tobacco, the only commodity they have to purchase. Only two thousand of these ancient nomadic hunters survive. The Hazda have resisted attempts by the government to persuade them to abandon their traditional ways. The local Hazda chief, Hasari, took us on a hike to his village of a few grass huts. The huts have to be replaced every year. A withered crone, almost blind, sat quietly, crouched in a corner by a fire. A tall, attractive young woman with big dark eyes and high shiny cheekbones had a languid five-month-old at her breast and a sick two-year-old at her feet. The infant stared weakly and was not responsive. Both children were dehydrated, malnourished and had severe respiratory tract infections. Flies nestled in the secretions coming from their eyes and nose.

John asked me, "You're a doctor. Can you help?"

"John, they need immediate medical care, more than I can give them," I lamented. The nearest doctor was thirty miles away, a two-day walk that would certainly have killed both babies. I was heartsick because they would die if they didn't get immediate medical care. John responded to my concerns and had them driven to the hospital. When they returned the next day, the children's eyes were bright, focused and responsive. Their skin tone glowed from rehydration as they proudly showed me the week's worth of medication they'd been given to continue their recovery.

That night we slept lightly in our simple camp, often awakened by scurrying field mice. Karen, more afraid of rodents than lions, accepted the mice as long as they didn't enter our tightly zipped tent. She realized she was the intruder in their environment, unlike the detested mice that try to enter our house back home for the winter. Jackals brayed close by. We felt vulnerable, but snuggled together for safety.

A bumpy five-hour drive took us to what was described as the wildlife jewel of the trip, the Ngorongoro Crater. Our hotel overlooked the crater and we descended into it by 8:30 the next morning. We popped the top of the Land Rover and immediately saw herds of buffalo, hordes of wildebeests, thousands of Tommy gazelles and zebras, hundreds of flamingoes, and a few elephants. The thousands of animals were overwhelming but so close together it felt like we were at the San Diego Wild Animal Park. Suddenly, a whisper between drivers and John took off as fast as he could over the bumpy road. Four-wheel drive vehicles sped from all corners of the park to the same clearing. Two large, adolescent male lions were sleeping deeply with their engorged abdomens pumping up and down. Skins scarred by many battles for their own survival, they had just eaten their fill and were dozing off a heavy meal. Their frightening wide-mouthed yawn amazed us when they stretched and slowly rose between the cars. A nearby SUV spun its wheels, stuck in thick mud.

John said, "I'm getting out to push that car." Adam pleaded, "Don't do it, John," but John said, "I've got to!"

John left the car and helped the stalled vehicle out of the mud while another car blocked the lions from seeing him. We knew the lions could smell him, but they were content with their recent meal and John probably knew that. With John getting out of the car, we became brave enough to roll down our windows to get better pictures.

Not much later, we observed a pride of four lionesses from afar. We had seen so many lions by this time we didn't even linger to gaze from a distance. I can't believe this, I thought, I'm already passing up seeing lions in the wild.

A few miles away we found two baby spotted hyenas outside of their cave. In contrast to their parents, who possess the strongest jaws of all land predators, the babies were playful, sweet creatures. We were surprised that the hyena mother didn't come out of the cave to protect her young. Female hyenas are aggressive and have been known to bite off the face of a person sleeping outside, even when not provoked.

The next morning we made another early descent into the Ngorongoro Crater. The Land Rover tore down the bumpy road for half a mile until we saw a cheetah on the prowl. It alternated between a trotting pace and slowly stalking a herd of Thompson gazelles. The cat let out a high-pitched bird-like call, shifting into a long loping run toward the Tommies. Suddenly, the cheetah extended each stride to over 20 feet until she flew at 70 miles per hour. The Land Rover followed at half speed and the herd of Tommies took off. We lost the predator in the brush just as it made its kill and the dust kicked up by other cars blocked our view. We realized we had gone too far, so John raced the car in reverse until we were finally able to see a filtered view of the cheetah devouring the Tommy.

We shifted our focus to the historic Olduvai Gorge, an hour away from the Ngorongoro Crater. The gorge is one of the richest archeological sites in the world and quite a different experience from the big cats. It contains layers dating back four million years of animal and human ancestral life. About three million years ago, three upright hominids, the first animals to walk upright, and a predecessor of the horse, walked the Laetoli Plain. A volcanic eruption covered their tracks with ash, preserving their footprints. Primitive tools, animal bones, and the skull of *homo habilis* were also found in the gorge dating back one to two million years ago. Still another set of million-year-old animal bones, including the skull of our direct ancestor, *homo erectus*, was found here. Adam pressed his face against the glass case containing the bones, fascinated though he was frightened of skulls.

The manager of the nearby Ndutu Lodge told us a few days before our arrival an elephant and a pride of lions had passed through the grounds. We were advised to be cautious in venturing beyond the groomed areas, particularly Adam and Jack, as they could easily become lion food. Fortunately, only a solitary giraffe nibbled on trees just in front of us while we ate lunch. We hiked with a forest ranger carrying a submachine gun. I wondered why he was armed until he pointed out the fresh tracks of lions. He motioned to Adam to stay close by and taught him to recognize the hoof prints and scat or feces of many of these animals. Karen and I teased Adam about how rapidly he was able to memorize scat.

We left our charming Ndutu hotel for Serengeti National Park, the size of the state of Connecticut. Shortly after entering we saw two cheetahs resting a few feet from the road. They stood up, stretched and walked next to the car, rubbing against each other's bodies in cat-like fashion. I showed Adam the beautiful dark lines that circle the cheetah's eyes and follow the edge of the nose to the corner of its mouth.

On the road to the northern section of the Serengeti, there were groups of animals on either side of us. At one site I saw many baboons and giraffes on my left and more than 30 elephants and a pair of vultures feasting on a wildebeest carcass on my right. We checked into a safari lodge where a man armed with bow and arrow escorted us back and forth to our room. We heard lions roaring at dinner and through the night, but they lived across the river and the water was too deep for them to cross, or so the owners of the hotel told us. For all the elegance and security, we wondered if the staff really could protect us if a lion prowled the camp.

Adam's enthusiastic appreciation of everything we saw greatly pleased me. I hoped he'd stay this way forever and not enter a phase of adolescent cool where excitement is forbidden and my enthusiasm is dismissed as utterly stupid. I believed this because of, or in spite of, raising two older sons.

Two years later, we took our second and less structured trip to a more untouched part of Africa, and realized then how protected we had been on our first adventure. As Adam grew older and Karen and I became more seasoned, we took risks necessary to experience more of the continent, its wildlife and people, its poverty and political discord. Nevertheless, there was tantalizing danger in Tanzania and our first safari was a good teacher. We learned how proper structure could permit us to take Adam anywhere in the world.

6

BACK TO AFRICA

Botswana, Zimbabwe—Summer 2003

KAREN, ADAM, NOW NINE, AND I were the only passengers on a single-engine plane as it scooted toward a private landing field in the Okavonga Delta in Botswana.

When we attempted to land, elephants scrambled away in every direction. We buzzed them off the runway, circled the area and were able to touch down on our second approach. Our guide, David, greeted us and we drove off in a roofless Land Cruiser—even the windshield was braced down flat against the hood. There were no barriers between the animals and us. We were suddenly treated to herds of elephants, hippos, and small antelopes called *lechwe* just outside our camp.

Our family was alone with every animal that we saw that day; there were no other tourists. David drove us to a deserted watering hole, looked at us with piercing blue eyes, and in the almost-British accent of a white Zimbabwean said, "Slow down, expect nothing, and enjoy the peacefulness."

We tentatively left the car, waited and stretched when suddenly on our right coming toward us was a large herd of elephants, mainly protective females and their Dumbo-sized babies. Adam, a veteran of a prior African safari but still thin and without recognizable muscles, asked David if we should get back in the car. "No," he answered, "just stay still and feel welcome in their space."

On our left, another herd marched single file, appearing one by one through the dense brush. All at once, two more herds tramped in and about 70 elephants surrounded us. Several females bleated and fanned their ears in a mock charge. David relieved our fears, encouraging us to just take it all in. We stood by the car, not hopping in or closing the door for fear of startling the herds of elephants drinking, snorting, and peeing all around us. For the moment, Karen, Adam, and I, with the aid of David, were quietly merged with dozens of three-ton beasts.

Dusk came quickly as the sun fell below the acacia trees, and when it was totally dark we switched on our spotlight and began our night game-drive back to camp. David taught us to recognize the eyes of crocodiles and hippos that were reflected in our light. We arrived at camp content with our first few hours with David and the Moremi Game

Reserve. I had barely enough time to wash up for dinner when Timba, our waiter, shouted that a lion had just passed through the camp. We hopped back into the Land Cruiser and turned on the night beam. David showed us the lion tracks and handed the light to Adam to follow them as he drove. The freshness of the tracks revealed we were getting closer and closer. The first powerful lioness popped out of the brush. Two more mighty females came and finally a young male. The pair of lionesses brushed by and greeted the first, like women touching cheeks at a cocktail party.

We parked and watched, using the illumination of our camcorder to shoot stills of the lions' interactions. David told Adam: "Be still so that the lionesses will not be able to distinguish you from the car and see you as a potential, juicy little meal." As ferocious as these beasts were, their sienna-colored skin and contented smile reminded us of our yellow Labrador retriever back home. Our family had never before seen a pride of lions without a bunch of cars to compete with. Famished and happy, we returned to our camp for dinner, a meal featuring home-baked rolls, soup, and skewered chicken, topped off with an excellent South African chardonnay.

I was amazed at the differences between Botswana and Tanzania. For the past two years Adam had often asked, "When can we go back to Africa?"

"One day," I would reply, "it's very expensive," to

which Adam would respond, "We could use a credit card."

Then a friend who had been to Africa many times gave me Mark Nolting's book *Africa's Top Wildlife Countries 1997* for a birthday gift. Another friend had been to South Africa and Botswana with her ten-year-old son and brought back astounding pictures and stories. We called the travel group founded by Nolting, the Africa Adventure Company, and decided to fly into South Africa and tour Botswana and Zimbabwe on a single-family tour during the summer of 2003.

The trip began in Johannesburg at the Grace Hotel in the suburb of Rosebank. We walked to a flea market through a direct passageway from our hotel. After hearing so many frightening things about Jo-berg, I was shocked at how safe I felt there. I gave Adam a few dollars and he budgeted and bargained—he was exhilarated by his purchase of a malachite crocodile for less than two dollars.

Our lodging in Botswana was in a mobile-tented camp, where our two 12-by-16-foot tents had surprisingly comfortable single beds, a private bucket shower, and a toilet for each tent. At night we heard the calls of lions, the *whhhuppps* of hyenas, and the grunts of hippos. David was tantalized by the roars of the lions and determined to find them the next morning. We woke at 6:30, donned our warmest layers of clothing and covered ourselves with coarse blankets in the cool morning and wind exposure of an open vehicle. We followed the lion tracks in our car for an hour until Dave got out his rifle and said it was time to track the lion on foot. He showed us how to follow the tracks and tell how recently the lions had gone by, using the depth and clarity of their prints. We saw marks in the sand left by the lions' swishing tails. Dave let Adam use the GPS to guide us back to the car after a two-hour walk did not result in sighting a lion.

Returning to the car, we walked along the Khwari River, until just the other side of a bend we saw three large lionesses. We watched them for about an hour as they barely moved, and Dave's enthusiasm for gazing was infectious. We all sat quietly as Dave, like Animal Planet's Crocodile Hunter, explained the lion's movements. "You can see their power even though they are resting," he whispered. "Look at those muscles."

A large troop of baboons sauntered down to the water in front of us during our lunch of Adam's favorite food—spaghetti. At the onset of our evening game drive, Adam nagged Dave to get back to the lions, but we stopped at another watering hole to watch the elephants. The babies were nursing and climbing all over their older siblings. Contrary to the old adage about being as noisy as a bunch of elephants, the herd moved stealthily and silently. The elephants, or ellies as the guides called them, rolled in the mud after their drink and dried off in the dust. Female elephants, like the lionesses, repeatedly rubbed and touched each other and their babies. Thick dust blew across the water to our vehicle, bringing a blended odor of elephant, dirt, and water that was so rich and fecund we could taste it.

The next morning, we moved our entire mobile camp into the Moremi Game Reserve where we would no longer be able to track on foot, drive off-road, or take night drives. We met a solitary man in a Land Rover going in the opposite direction from us just after we entered Moremi. He was interested in viewing lions so Dave told him exactly where he could find them. When Dave asked if he'd seen anything interesting, he replied, "There's a leopard up a tree at the hippo pool."

We headed there as fast as we could go on the sandy, bumpy road. Dave knew exactly where to find the leopard. He pointed to a knobby vine spiraling up a tree and to the tail of a leopard that ran along the vine. I followed the vine to the tail and the tail to a vertical branch upon which sat a splendid leopard of about 150 pounds. We watched it sit on the branch for an hour as the sun arched its way over the leopard's head. Dave speculated that when the direct sun hit the leopard's eyes, it would leave the tree for shade. We sat quietly as Dave whispered enthusiastically, "I could watch it all day!"

Karen persuaded Dave to leave for lunch and come back later when there would be a chance of seeing it in different light. We had cheese and chutney sandwiches by the hippo lake before we returned to the leopard and were treated to a full view of its extended body. I felt excitedly vulnerable to its full pounce in our open car when it stretched out, but we were all too busy snapping pictures to worry.

In my tent that night, I listened to the sounds of elephants chomping and tree branches crashing, which were getting louder as the elephants got closer. Lions called to each other from opposite sides of the campsite with roars and deep rumbling growls, tempting Dave to try to find them the next day. Although they sounded very close, maybe too close, Dave told us their roars could be heard as far as six miles away.

Adam and I slept soundly and right through a visit to our tents by a large hyena that leaned against the mesh with its eyes only a few feet from Karen's. She used the mantra she had learned from Dave to calm her and not show fear. "You respect my space and I'll respect yours. You have your place and I have mine. I won't hurt you and you won't hurt me." The hyena slowly backed away, and an hour later Karen heard the anguished squeals of a kill, leaving her too anxious to sleep. Dave confirmed that the hyena's forepaw tracks were only a few feet from Karen's tent that night.

The next morning, and for years to come whenever she told the story, Karen spoke of her response to the hyena without screaming in fear as a profound emotional triumph.

Dave, who taught Adam how to recognize hyena spoor, took us on a mission to find the lions he'd heard the night before, but first we watched a pair of busybody jackals roaming and sniffing in a wheat-colored field. Finally we spotted two lionesses on either side of a termite mound. We viewed them from afar because national park rules prohibited us from driving off-road to get closer.

Dave told us two more hyenas at the campsite awakened him but Karen slept soundly through the night. After a hearty breakfast we left on our last drive with Dave, who would take us to meet our plane.

We met a South African couple on our way out of camp. They told us that a cheetah had just passed over the bridge moments before we crossed. They showed us their video of a baboon chasing our favorite big cat into dense sage, where they lost sight of it. Dave went on a mission to find the wily cheetah, driving frenetically back and forth until he spotted it, a tiny dot in the landscape about a quarter mile away. I followed its head, barely moving, until I saw a baboon chase it into a resting spot in the sage.

An elephant walked toward the cheetah and Dave whispered in his Animal Hunter voice "When the elephant gets close to the cheetah, it will stir and we will see it again." The cheetah stood in full glory, just as he predicted, and circled back in front of us. Suddenly it raced after a warthog family at sixty miles an hour. The male warthog took off, leaving the mother to protect her baby. The cheetah chased them into the bush and moments later, the mother escaped. Dave said that the mother's leaving meant the baby must have been killed. This was our second cheetah kill, and

John, our guide on our first safari, told us he hadn't seen one in ten years. Dave, Adam, and I were pumped about our experience of the chase. Karen was relieved that she didn't see the kill. Dave kept repeating, "Oh happy day! What luck!" He was sweating now, and we all peeled off our morning layers of clothing.

The three of us checked into our hotel in Victoria Falls and immediately went to the Zambezi riverbank for a sundown cocktail cruise. Shortly after we left the dock, we saw several large herds of elephants cross the deep, wide river by a combination of walking on rocks and paddling. From the safety of the boat, we were able to come closer than ever to a crocodile.

After the cruise, Adam and I ate smoked crocodile at dinner and it tasted like smoked tuna. Adam also had warthog, which he said was as good as any pork he had ever eaten.

The next morning I left alone for my rafting trip on the very dangerous Zambezi. I dreamt about my deceased father for the first time, and it felt like he was summoning me to join him. I didn't share the dream with Karen lest she try to dissuade me from going. Adam was seven years too young for the river trip so he and Karen spent the day exploring The Falls and shopping. My tour package included a huge English breakfast, which I declined. Breakfast for me was a time to figure out the group of paddlers I would try to join.

My friend Cappy had done this trip a year ago and shouted with joy when he showed me an exhilarating videotape of one of the greatest adventures of his life. Cappy advised me to get on a boat with huge, muscular South African or Australian guys to minimize the chances of the almost inevitable capsizing in the hippo and crocodile-infested river. As hard as I tried, I couldn't connect with the big Australians, but I had a very interesting conversation about the role of pharmaceutical companies with Greg, an American medical ethicist. Greg told me he had a second job in the summer—a whitewater rafting guide. He chose me for his group so I didn't hesitate to sign the usual rafting disclaimer that I would not hold the Shearwater Company responsible in the event of my death or dismemberment.

We piled into a rusted yellow school bus and drove to a bluff from which we descended 600 vertical feet to the river. We launched our rafts at rapid 11, and would miss those with names like Stairway to Heaven, Devil's Toilet Bowl, Commercial Suicide, and Gnashing Jaws of Death. I wondered how they thought of so many frightening names. The most disturbingly named rapid that awaited me was Terminator, but Oblivion and The Last Straw didn't sound too comforting either.

Greg had picked the rest of his crew, including two rafters from Idaho. We were dressed in helmets, wetsuit tops, and snug life jackets. Our guide Pan drilled us in four simple commands: "Forward," "Backward," "Stop," and "Hold On." The latter meant get down on your knees, grab your paddle, and grip the rope that circles the boat. When we had mastered these commands he called, "Faster, Faster, Faster" and "Together!" Pan had us jump off the boat at a spot where no hippos or crocs were to be seen and climb back up or be hauled in. Greg dragged me up by my vest, and the dunking relieved some of my fears about falling in the water. Five skillful kayakers, four for rescue and one videographer, accompanied us. They reminded me of hip hop dancers as they performed 360-degree spins and bopped upstream.

Our first rapid was Overland Truck Eater, and when we entered it we were immediately struck by three huge waves coming at us from all sides. We stayed on through this triple rollercoaster while paddlers on other boats were tossed into the river, though easily rescued by the expert kayakers. We toasted our success with a rafter's high five, connecting oars at the center of the boat.

I was too frightened on the larger rapids to enjoy the beauty of the river; my only focus was survival. Waves kept knocking me to the bottom of the boat, but each time I sprang back up in a vain attempt to paddle. On Oblivion, a grade V, I bounced up in time to catch one of our own paddlers by his dangling foot and jerk him in before he fell overboard.

After a lunch stop, everyone relaxed for the last three

calmer rapids and splashed each other in mock battles. The boats emptied us onto the shore for the most vertical climb I had ever undertaken. It seemed as formidable as Half Dome in Yosemite. Struggling up the steep slope while using my paddle as a walking stick, I was spurred on by knowing that replenishing fluids awaited me at the summit. When I reached it, I drank a bottle of water and a beer, each with a single gulp. I had survived despite my late father's beckoning me. I did not join the three people who die on the Zambezi every year.

The Zulu name for Victoria Falls, *Mosi oa Tunya*, means "The smoke that thunders," based on the constant mist it hurls into the air and the booming sound that echoes throughout the town. I was struck by the huge mass of raging, cascading waters framed by a series of rainbows arching over each section of the falls. It is said that when David Livingstone first saw the falls in 1855 he said, "On sights as beautiful as this, angels in their flight must have gazed." He named the falls Victoria after his queen.

During our stay in Zimbabwe the currency was in inflationary chaos. When we checked out, the hotel calculated our $125-per-night bill at 800 Zimbabwe dollars to one American dollar, cutting our bill in half. Stores sold their goods at 2,000 Zim to the dollar and one week after we left Vic Falls, we were told that it took 4,000 Zim to obtain one U.S. dollar. Zimbabweans had to spend so much time waiting at banks for currency of dwindling value that there was little time to do anything else.

Hwange National Park, Zimbabwe

Our lodge in Hwange Park was less than an hour by bush plane from Vic Falls. Game drives were rewarding in our private section of the park. A herd of buffalo turned, faced off against a lion, and it backed away. A pride of lionesses with eight cubs passed a buffalo leg back and forth, and another lion guarded its fresh wildebeest kill for three days until it gave it away to a flock of at least fifty vultures.

Herds of antelopes including kudu, steenbok and sable were abundant, but our most challenging experience occurred when we sat by the tiny hotel pool on a sultry afternoon. Adam saw a herd of elephants in the distance and said, "They are coming to drink at the pool." When I said, "No, they are coming to the water hole," he responded with "If I splash the water to sound like a waterfall, they will come here to drink."

Soon twenty elephants approached as we sat by the pool and the three of us were stone-scared. No one else was around, and we knew cow elephants are so protective of their babies that they can swat a human adult with their trunk and gore him to death with their tusks. Somehow we watched them get closer and closer. We barely flinched.

David's message rang in our ears: "Sit calmly and respect their space and they will respect yours." Twenty elephant trunks reached over the edge of the pool and began sucking in water. The large ellies were monstrous. The smaller ones stood on tiptoes and the ends of their trunks barely reached the water. Hardly breathing, we picked up our cameras and started shooting videos and close-up stills, the elephants' trunks only inches from our feet. Back home, no one would believe this. Daring to not move more than a twitch, we contained our fear and exhilaration until after they lumbered away. With a whoop and a holler, Adam ran to tell the hotel staff about how the elephants drank half the water in the pool and how close they'd been. I wanted to join him and shout about our achievement but held back, hugging and high-fiving Karen, celebrating just between us.

We had learned to be calm among the wild animals, even when inches away and without a guide. I was shocked that our most memorable experience had taken place right by our lodge. We were beginning to understand the message of Africa: peak experiences most often come to you when you least expect them.

Motopos Hills, Zimbabwe

We flew in a single-engine plane to the Bulawayo airstrip. The pilot offered us a copy of *The Daily News*, Zimbabwe's only private daily newspaper, which reported that lines in banks for cash were endless and that President

Robert Mugabe was dealing with the problem of inflation by printing bills of larger denominations. Cash shortages were due not only to rampant inflation but also because the government could not afford the special ink and paper needed to print bank notes. Two months after our trip, the Zimbabwe government shut down *The Daily News*.

Phillip, owner of the Amalinda Hotel, picked us up with the warm greeting, "We haven't seen American tourists here in three years." A warning about Zimbabwe was posted on the U.S. Traveler's Advisory list, but African Adventures Tours assured us it was safe to travel in this country, which, despite its politics, has the best safari guides.

He introduced us to our guide, whose name was Never because his family never thought they'd have a boy. He spoke eight African languages, including a click dialect of the San Bushmen that sounded like an Eartha Kitt scat. Phil and his wife, Sharon, were candid about how their family had suffered as a result of Mugabe's policies and personal greed. Sharon's father, like many white landowners, had recently had his farm taken away from him at gunpoint by Mugabe followers who, when they took over, had no idea about how to farm the land. (Many white farmers were killed and most blacks were starving.)

Never took us on a rhino hunt at Motopos National Park. As we entered, he apologized for the deterioration of the park, explaining that most of the money allocated for fences, roads, and clearing had been diverted to Mugabe's private use. As a result of this neglect, many of the animals were gone, but we had a good chance of seeing rhinos.

Never spotted two pairs of white rhinos, each a cow and its calf. He pulled the car over and we crept toward them. Karen's body and teeth shook with fear as we approached one pair, while the other two were only about thirty feet to our right. Never whispered that we'd be okay as long as we stayed downwind. "But winds change!" I protested. The rhinos turned toward us, by now only ten feet away. Karen asked Never if we could move back, but he pointed to the oxpecker and fork-tailed drongo on top of the rhino and said, "The birds are not afraid. Why should you be scared?"

A wedding party joined Adam, Karen, and I at breakfast. The groom had left his job as a guide on hunting safaris to manufacture furniture. Never, who had worked with the groom in the past, also joined us. The groom's white father challenged him, "When is your president going to step down?" Never shifted uncomfortably in his chair, stood up, poured coffee for Karen and replied, "Mugabe has killed thousands of my people. He will be eighty soon and I hope he will retire then, as the law requires."

We visited a local Ndebele family, where the man of the house had two wives. The senior wife was grinding corn meal while the junior spouse was picking corn off the cob and putting it into sacks. Never told us the junior one, who appeared about fifty years old, was the medicine woman with whom we had requested a visit. She left us to change into her medicine woman clothing, and when she returned I realized she had an opaque film covering her yellow-green eyes. She wore porcupine quills on her head and the pelts of several animals on her body.

The medicine woman sat on a goatskin on which she placed a spear, a bent stick, and the tail of a wildebeest. We eagerly waited for her to go into a trance, but Never told us that she could not do it because she had already eaten a meal and trances were only possible before breakfast or in the late evening. We sat before her for almost an hour and spoke with the aid of Never's translation. Karen felt a strong connection when the Ndebele woman asked her if she, too, were a medicine woman from the West.

"Kind of," Karen replied. "I work with emotional problems like anxiety and depression." The woman nodded knowingly and replied, "So do I." Karen told her she had a calming presence and asked her, "How did you become a medicine woman?"

"A medicine man told me I had a special energy," she replied. "For years, he asked me if he could train me and I kept saying no. Gradually, I became blind. He said that he could heal me, but only if I became a medicine woman. I agreed and he taught me rituals that slowly returned my sight over many months. He showed me how to use herbs and trance and by the time I could see again, I had become a medicine woman."

Karen gave her a beaded bracelet she'd purchased in New Zealand and the medicine woman was thrilled. Karen kept a twin to the bracelet and they shared a look that meant their connection would continue.

We had dinner at Sharon and Phillip's cozy home that night, where we learned that Sharon's brother had left the country over fear of Mugabe's policy towards whites and his overall ruin of the country. Her brother sold his share of the hotel to Sharon and Phil and left for Namibia. When Phil talked about why he was staying, he sounded to me like the Jews in Germany in 1938.

"I love my country," he said. "The situation will get better when Mugabe retires in a year or so. Sharon has to be near her father. When trade embargoes were placed on my country for apartheid, we developed the ability to grow or manufacture everything ourselves that we had previously imported."

When the Blacks rebelled against the Whites over twenty years ago, Sharon and her female friends learned to shoot and drive cars at the age of twelve. Sharon and Phillip, who have been independent most of their lives, were not ready to give up their businesses and leave the country.

A year after our safari, we learned that Mugabe had postponed his commitment to step down until 2008. Almost two years later, on April 3, 2005, I read a *Los Angeles*

Times headline: "Mugabe Plans to Rule Until Age of 100."

In July of 2005, Mugabe bulldozed the homes of 1.5 million Zimbabwean blacks in a one-month period, causing rampant instant homelessness. He claimed it was long overdue slum clearance and refused to accept an offer from an international agency of thirty million dollars to relocate the 1.2 million Zimbabweans who were still homeless in November 2005. In September of that year, Hwange had a terrible drought, its national parks service had no funds for diesel fuel for the water pumps, and without water at least thirty animals were dying every day. Perhaps a tourist, traveling with his family on safari, has no right or sufficient information to judge a third world nation's leader. But what I heard and saw when I was in Zimbabwe and what I read after I returned led me to feel strongly that Mugabe was a self-serving dictator who neglected the needs of all but a few citizens of his country.

Adam had confronted poverty at the market, remained calm in the presence of lions, and not backed down from a troop of baboons. He had survived two weeks without peers and not shed a single tear. Karen had looked a hyena in the eye, stood ten feet from four rhinos, and befriended a medicine woman. She had learned that it was worth braving latrines and cold showers if adventures awaited her. I had survived being thrown about like a rag doll by the turbulent waters of the Zambezi despite a warning from my deceased father. All three of us sat toe to trunk with a herd of elephants and had not flinched except to click our cameras. The good people of Zimbabwe who had guided us through our triumphs have yet to successfully challenge the monarch Mugabe, who squashes all dissent.

7

A Home By The Sea

Laguna Beach, 1983

I DRIVE UP THE HILL to my canyon view house on Old Top Of The World Drive, my left arm limp in a sling. I broke my collarbone the day before while bodysurfing to show off to another woman while my wife watched from a distance. The other woman, not my wife, drove me to the E.R. I thought about how much I love the ocean. I often dreamt of living close enough to walk from home and swim every day. I slowly open the front door with my unencumbered hand. Ellen, my wife of 24 years, seems more uptight than usual. Her hands are shaking and her jaw trembling.

"I want you to leave as soon as you can," she said, out of what seemed like nowhere to me at the time, yet I realized what a jerk I'd been when I thought about it several weeks later.

Too shocked to respond, I finally rasped, "When?"

"Soon!" was all she could say.

I got what I wished for, a small beachfront pad. I made the sparse rooms as homey as I could, taking with me an old Tibetan prayer rug and a few abstract paintings. The haunting green chairs were long gone by now, but I loved that gold and brown rug for its braided, bright colors that never seem to fade. I placed the carpet in the center of the small 'great' room where it led my gaze towards floor-to-ceiling windows framing the ocean. Neither the soothing sounds of the waves nor the comfort of my sons sleeping over helped me sleep later than 4 a.m. I wrote a self-help book for spouses of alcoholics in the early morning until the light of dawn let me run on the beach or collect driftwood for my simple fireplace.

When my winter lease expired, I purchased a house halfway up the hill, just a block away from my son Tony's intermediate school. I moved my rug and paintings in, but it wasn't a home. I tried to break away from my girlfriend, but each time I found myself lured back. After several chaotic years, I was finally able to let go and convince both of us it was over. Friends had been trying to fix me up with Karen ever since she moved to L.A. from Arizona shortly after my divorce, so I was really looking forward to meeting her.

I folded a beige silk handkerchief into the pocket

of my double-breasted suit jacket that perfectly matched the pattern of my tie and took her to dinner at the finest place in town. I was uneasy about our moving together to a rock beat so I waited for a slow song for our first dance. The moment I felt her body push and fold into me all full and warm and I let her sensual smile and soothing voice take me in, it was all over. I was toast, putty, and chicken schmaltz all at once.

That night we interviewed each other, not merely as clinicians, but as soul mates sensing we might be partners for life. Karen's key question for me was, "Would you have another child?"

My critical query, less complicated, "Will you watch the Lakers with me, the whole game?"

We agreed to these basic issues. I happily postponed my empty nest for another eighteen years, but she stopped watching basketball after Magic Johnson left the sport.

When Karen came to the house for the first time, my research assistant and Tony were living there, and my oldest son Alex and several of his friends were in the hot tub drinking beer. All Karen had to say was "Yikes" and I knew how she felt about my ménage. By the time she moved in, only Tony was there.

We slowly began to know each other now that we had committed to one another. We easily agreed on spending and saving money, lifestyle, books, dancing, jazz, and not eating red meat. We reconciled her Catholicism and my Judaism with a gradual mutual movement towards Buddhism. We never resolved timeliness and neatness. I'm early. She's late. I'm a bit sloppy. She's quite neat. She thinks I'm messy, I think she's compulsive.

A few months after Karen moved in with me she overheard me speaking about MY house. That statement and a battle with rats that lived in the palm trees next to us was enough for Karen, who said, "Let's look for OUR home now."

We found one, close to the ocean. I laid out my carpets, Karen adopting the prayer rug for her meditation area. After Adam was born, we added a new master bedroom cantilevered over a creek, near enough to the sea for me to be lulled to sleep by crashing waves and Karen's contented presence.

8

FEH!
(WHITEY, THE DAD WITH THE DAGGY CIGAR)
Philadelphia

WHEN I WAS EIGHT YEARS OLD, my father took me to my first Phillies' baseball game. He bought me a hot dog and a Coke. "Can I have another hot dog to go with the rest of my Coke?" I pleaded. He leaned over me, chewing on juicy pieces of his soggy cigar. My mother called it daggy. I later learned that this word means the dung that mats into the fleece surrounding a sheep's anus and hangs in dried, dangling clumps, an image that closely resembled the pulp of his cigar. I wondered how my mom knew about this expression from New Zealand.

"Watch the game, son," he demanded, "that's why we're here, not to eat." He taught me how to keep a line score of the game—six-four-three, double play. This was the last skill I let him teach me.

He put up a basketball net in our seven-foot ceilinged basement and told Mom he was showing me how to play. At 5 feet 5 inches he was a foot taller and 100 pounds heavier. He backed me in slowly, pushing me into the wall right under the basket, then turned and dunked. When I attempted my two-handed shots he swatted them away years before I knew this was goal tending and not allowed.

My father had been a pitcher for a semi-professional team called Defiant's Pro. I wore his grossly oversized uniform one Halloween and neighbors asked, "Are you Whitey Kaufman's son?" I trembled with excitement when he offered to teach me the secret of a curve ball. He tried to show me how to grip the ball and turn my wrist, but after a few tries, he grunted, "*feh*," a Yiddish word of disapproval, spat out a dag, and headed for home.

Dad attempted to show me how to ride a bicycle when I was nine. I fell several times during the short lesson and was met with, "FEH, you'll never get it." It took four years until I finally learned, and then easily from a group of my friends.

I prepared for my sixteenth birthday by saving money so I could purchase a learner's permit. Of course my father tried to teach me to drive and of course I panicked and of course he gave up on me with an ego-piercing "FEH."

My mother was fifty-three years old when she died. I tried to embrace my father at the funeral, but he froze and

Feh!

I dropped my arms rather than hug an icicle. He remarried, very quickly, to Esther, a woman who passed away twenty years later. Dad became impotent from prostate problems and developed the delusion that whenever she was away, she was indulging in wild lesbian orgies. Actually she was gambling in Atlantic City and when her faculties slipped she lost all her winnings and more.

My sister and I spent the night in his apartment the evening following her funeral. He insisted that I sleep with him. "It's OK, Eddie," he pleaded. "I'm not like Esther." At last, he had attempted to be close to me, but this time I experienced, but did not announce, the powerful "FEH" permeating my every pore.

A decade or so later my sister called and said, "Dad's dying. Come to Florida right away!" He was in a coma when I arrived and Glenda asked me to stay with him so she could get some sleep.

I spoke to Dad, hoping to break through his coma, and told him I was here with him now. I covered myself with a blanket and lay on the reclining chair beside him. My breathing shifted to a half-beat synchronicity with his, and after a few hours I fell asleep. Suddenly, I was awakened by the awareness that he had stopped breathing. He had waited until I was with him to die.

9

Wedding In Saraburi

Thailand, 2003

Christmas morning, 2003. Orange Alert! screamed the headlines of the *L.A. Times*. Six Air France planes to Los Angeles International Airport canceled! LAX under heavy suspicion of terrorist act! Karen, nine-year-old Adam, and I were traveling to Bangkok that evening. My oldest son, Alex, was to marry a Thai woman in a Buddhist temple 60 miles north of the Bangkok airport in two days.

Getting to LAX and checking in turned out to be easy, despite all the warnings and security precautions. I have never seen so many policemen in an airport. We had dinner at the Daily Grill in the International Terminal, where there were at least 100 policemen. We wondered if there were any left to patrol the airport.

We changed planes in Hong Kong, where the airport

was on alert as a result of a recent case of SARS in China. Viruses and terrorist threats plagued us on this trip.

The three of us passed easily through Thai customs and immigration and started looking for Alex, and easily spotted him towering over all the Thai taxi drivers. Alex is thin, athletic, and ruggedly handsome with long eyelashes framing striking blue eyes. He has the relaxed demeanor of a California surfer, but the anxiety about getting places on time shared by all the males in my family. It never ceases to amaze me that he's been living in Thailand since 1996.

Alex concentrated on getting us out of the airport as quickly as possible. I could feel his body tense up and emit a message of "let's get on the road" when we embraced. Alex filled us in on the parties and ceremonies that awaited us. In the back seat Adam whispered to Karen, "Three ceremonies! I hope they're not too boring."

We went straight to the luncheon party without changing or showering, expecting everyone would already be there. We were the first to arrive, so Adam and I whipped out our bathing suits and dove into a cool gurgling stream by a waterfall just in front of our picnic site. As I emerged from the water, a white van pulled up to the restaurant across from the lake and several of my family members got out. Suddenly, I felt like Scrooge confronted by the Ghost of Christmas Past. I had not seen my sister, Glenda, or ex-wife, Elle, in years. Elle's brother, my son Tony, their spouses, and Narm, Alex's bride to be, followed close behind them.

The main course was fresh river fish prepared steamed as well as barbecued with a sauce made from the fish's natural roe. It even passed Elle's watchful, critical culinary eye. Elle and I reminisced for the first time since the divorce. We spoke of how eating fresh fish in Asian sauces had been one of the memorable aspects of our past. We talked animatedly about past vacations together, but we were not aware of any hostility in our voices. Adam had been listening and had another view of our conversation. He often feels free to make statements about any and every topic.

"I know why you two got divorced," he said, "you disagree about everything." Shortly later he asked, "Who divorced who?" and I replied, "It was kind of mutual, Adam."

Tony overheard, but Elle didn't. He interjected, "No, Dad! It was Mom who decided to leave you."

I fell silent and thought about all the things I had done to provoke the divorce. I remembered the list of ten "non-negotiable demands" Elle had given me that had to be met if we were to reunite, and how I'd ripped them up after reading the first one. It requested that I not participate at all in her new catering business. I came out of my reverie and said, "Tony's right, Adam. It was his Mom's decision."

We returned to our hotel and checked out the facilities. Rooms were sparse but in an exotic tropical setting among brooks and waterfalls. Fields of sunflowers, many already gone to seed, surrounded the resort but there were still stretches of bright yellow flowers with big black dots in Van Gogh splendor. A shady trail under a dense forest canopy was signed Jurassic Park and led to a waterfall and swimming hole. Tony and Ariel, assigned the only room with a hot shower, generously gave it to us. This gift backfired a bit because during our stay many of the guests, including my sister but not Elle, borrowed our shower, giving the weekend the feeling of a Marx Brothers movie or French farce in which the cast of characters repeatedly go in and out of the same small bedroom or hotel room.

The first night my family was introduced to Narm's family at an elegant Thai dinner at the hotel. Narm looks like a mixture of a Thai orchid and Audrey Hepburn. She has a long, elegant neck, dark eyes and a creamy light tan complexion. Narm is the only member of her family who speaks English let alone the only college graduate. We could only communicate with her family by putting the tips of our hands together, raising them to our lips and bowing. They would respond with the same bow, called a *wai*.

A wedding celebration was held the second night accompanied by a 20-piece Thai orchestra. Several members of Narm's family approached mine and led us onto the dance floor, where they taught us how to perform Thai dances. Music and dance bridged our communication gap that night, but when the dancing stopped, the distance between the families returned like the fog slicing into our canyon back home.

Wedding in Saraburi

Alex and Narm's wedding ceremony seemed endless, lasting from early in the morning to late evening. We drove for over an hour to a Buddhist monastery for the first ceremony. The blue and salmon colored temple gate had a scalloped, multicolored triangle at the top. A small monkey in a saffron robe sat by the door, next to a monk who was smoking and talking on a cell phone, also dressed in saffron.

Alex was clad for his nuptials in a long maroon shirt outside of baggy black pants with a black and white sash draped from left shoulder to right hip. Narm was dressed elegantly but simply in a full length white dress, delicate white shawl and slim gold chain belt. Like everyone attending the ceremony, their shoes were left outside the temple.

The wedding party entered the temple and sat in a line facing the monks, with Alex at the head. Everyone lit a candle, several incense sticks, and made a wish, then waited for the monks to start chanting. They chanted for fifteen minutes, and when they stopped it was our signal to hand them their food. The monks avoided even the slightest eye contact with the women. Women are not permitted to touch the monks' bowls directly so they had to pick up and hand the monk a bowl using a cloth. Karen and I felt quite awkward during this ceremony but were guided through it by Narm's aunt, who seemed to be running the show.

The Second Ceremony was a traditional Welcoming of the Groom, held at the bride's family home where we formed a procession outside in the street. Alex walked in front with me on the left and his mother on his right. Two people stopped the groom with a "*Pratoo Ngern*" or Silver Gate. Alex paid a fee, then another to get through a Golden Gate ("*Pratoo Thong*"). Passing through these gates brings a rich future for the bride and groom. A third couple from the bride's family removed Alex's shoes. He stepped into Narm's home only after giving money to the gatekeepers. When this was accepted, it signified the bride's family's acceptance of Alex as their son.

Narm's family home was built like many in this area of Thailand to permit the first floor to be used as a shop. Not surprisingly, the living room was shop-like, sparsely furnished with shiny white walls. Alex whispered they'd worked hard to get it ready for the ceremony. When the initial glow of Alex's acceptance as their son wore off and we'd finished sharing the group photos of various combinations of the families, there was little to do but sit on the few chairs available and wonder if there would ever be much contact between the two families.

We returned to the hotel and headed right for the swimming hole. As we approached the falls, we heard the voices of Thai teenagers echoing up to us from the jungle walk. Alex told us they were local high school students and the musical entertainment for the wedding ceremony and party. Alex swam upstream with Adam on his back and dunked them both under the waterfall. Loving the rare closeness with his oldest brother and the thrill of being tossed, Adam asked Alex to do it again and again, and he did, to the tune of Adam's shrill cries and hoarse laughter.

The monks prepared a grassy area near the dining pavilion for the wedding ceremony. Prayer flags of red, white, green, blue, and yellow strung throughout the area formed an altar over three seated monks. The older one, who smoked during the ceremony, tossed his cigarette butts and an empty pack over his shoulder, behaviors not uncommon in Thai monks but that never cease to amaze me. They blessed Alex and Narm through a series of rituals said to bring the marital union good fortune. The eldest monk made a mark on the their foreheads with a holy white powder. Elle sat on Alex's right, holding his arm, and Narm's mom sat next to her as the monk blessed the newlyweds.

Sequenced by seniority, each guest tied a holy string around Alex and Narm's right arms till their upper limbs were covered in graying threads. Narm's grandmother tied them around the wrists of everyone in my family for good luck on our journey home, but we were told the string had to be kept on until it fell off. The wizened, heavily wrinkled grandma had blackened teeth, stained from chewing betel nuts like many of her generation. Narm's family approached Alex and Narm one by one and placed 500 baht notes under their strings, equivalent to $12.50, a lot of money to a rural Thai.

The high school band, consisting of twenty-five musicians who played Thai instruments, accompanied a dozen dancers that performed traditional movements with heads straight, hands elevated in the *om* position, and arms moving side to side. The bandleader's daughter, a tiny three-year-old, spun a wooden instrument resembling a large hamster exercise wheel. Many of the string instruments were elongated with only a string or two for strumming.

When the band switched to a rock and roll beat, the female members of Narm's family gently took each of us by the hand and taught us how to do modern Thai dancing. A young aunt instructed Karen and the "chief" aunt pulled Elle up to dance and wouldn't let her stop. Adam danced and played with several Thai girls who knew only a little English. Adam ran over to us and reported, "They said the F word!" I couldn't tell if he ran away from the girls in fear or glee. Dancing and *wais* were the only significant contact between the two families, and when the music stopped for the night I felt sad and wondered if we would ever have contact again.

My thrill at seeing my son married was only partially diminished by the distractions of seeing my ex-wife and the pageantry of the ceremony. Still, I had to step away from these powerful experiences and say to myself, "Amazing! Alex is married now—I never thought it would happen—and to a woman who combines the grace of a butterfly with an indomitable will."

10

After the Tsunami

Thailand, 2005

A Thai woman slumps into a chair in a daycare center next to the tin houses of Tung Kamin in southern Thailand. Her matted hair falls thickly below her shoulders. She carries a child's purse decorated with a cartoon of a smiling infant.

Her eyes glaze with a far away look as she wanders past bookshelves where children are playing. She stares at me and a slight smile lifts the corners of her mouth. It is not the broad welcoming Thai smile I am accustomed to. Karen asks Liz, the center's director, if she knows anything about this sad person.

Liz replies, "She was selling toothbrushes and toothpaste in a seaside village with her three children. Two were held close to her body by her sarong and a third played nearby. When the first wave of the tsunami hit, her children were ripped away. After the water receded, she saw them and called, 'I'll save you!' Suddenly the second wave came. Her children were pulled away and never seen again. When she can't sleep, which is often, she comes to my tent crying in the middle of the night until I hold her."

I questioned my confidence in Adam when he swam and surfed so confidently at the age of eleven. One powerful eight-footer back home and he could be lost in an instant. If I lost one of my sons, let alone all three, could I ever function again?

Karen, Adam, and I had returned to Thailand sixteen months after my oldest son Alex's wedding and a few months after the Tsunami struck Phuket. Alex and his wife, Narm, had established a center for Tsunami orphans in the devastated area of Tung Kamin. We sat on the floor with the children while Alex read *Green Eggs and Ham*, translating the melodious words into Thai. The older boys played non-verbal slapping-hands games with Adam, Karen, and me, followed by a foot wrestling game in our stocking feet.

The tsunami caused a devastating 5,395 deaths in Thailand. The loss of tourism that followed was called the Second Tsunami. Nevertheless, our last morning we awoke to a sunrise that filled the sky with clear blue light. As we left the hotel, we noticed that the tailor shop and restaurants around the hotel were opening for the first time since the tsunami. It was a new day in Phuket for the tourist and construction industries, but not for the villagers of Tung Kamin. Loss has left their families phantoms of who they were before the tragedy.

My son Alex's wedding brought back memories of the devastation of my own family as a result of divorce and how I had wandered around, a bit ghostlike for several years until I started my new clan. I was able to repair my personal damage and be reborn as husband and father. I wondered how many of the adults and children in Tung Kamin would ever be part of a family again.

11

The Blind Leading the Blind

Costa Rica, December 2004

GRUNTING CHANTS OF HOWLER MONKEYS rouse us at dawn from our tents on the sands of the Nicoya Peninsula in Costa Rica. Karen, ten-year-old Adam, and I, along with the other three families on the tour, prepare to kayak to Tortuga Island, about a mile off the beach.

The rich aroma of brewing dark Costa Rican coffee merges with the sultry tropical air. Each person in the group gets their own kayak and starts out across the bay, but a cooling breeze surprises us. Suddenly, the wind kicks up and the waves rise to at least six feet and come at us broadside. Adam and I instinctively tack directly into the wave. He is 100 feet ahead of me and dwarfed by the waves, but I hear him shouting, "Oh my God! Oh my God!" Karen's pedals are not adjusted properly; she is frustrated, angry, and out of control. She looks for Adam, but the waves are much taller than his head and she can only see the tip of his paddle. A wave buffets her from the side and she capsizes, but in no time a guide following Karen closely in a motorboat rescues her. He takes her to Tortuga Island to join the other families who wait on the sandy beach for her to arrive.

We crowd into a small dive boat to return to our campground. The driver takes us to the natural arch we had originally planned to paddle through, and throttles the boat all the way back to our base. The spray drenches us and I giggle when the warm water hits my face full force.

I was shocked to find out that a blind couple, Linda and James, were participants on this challenging adventure tour. Linda quickly confided in me that she and James are truly soul mates. They both have slowly progressive blindness and deafness. Linda was legally blind at forty and completely blind at the age of fifty, just a year before the Costa Rica trip, and at this time James still had a bit of sight and hearing. Linda walked mainly holding the shoulder of her daughter, Rachel, age nineteen, and James held on to Linda's sixteen-year-old son, David. Linda linked arms with James and he managed to steer them on a straight course. Linda quipped to me, "The blind leading the blind."

Rachel helped her mother to a chair, brought their lunch to the table and told her where the food was located.

"Rice, beans and chicken on the main plate, fruit juice at one o'clock, tortillas at ten o'clock." Rachel readily revealed that she is struggling with anorexia, obvious since her meals often consisted only of bowls of watermelon. David's eyes were barely open, giving him the appearance of being blind. Linda leaned close to me and rapidly whispered the secrets of her life: her abusive husband, divorce, suicide attempt, psychiatric hospitalization, and a pricey hearing implant that would be ruined if wet.

Following lunch, the group hiked in dim twilight while I brought up the rear with Linda and James. I was wearing my sunglasses and in the jungle darkness I could barely see better than he could. Howler monkeys greeted us with prolonged screeches as we entered camp. I barely made my way out of the jungle to the ocean as the sun set, with just enough light so I could spot a flying fish skipping goodbye to the day.

We drove from the sunny beach to our hotel in the rainforest the next morning and when we arrived a downpour pelted us. A four-hour kayak ride down the river was planned for the next morning and I was not looking forward to kayaking in the rain.

The next day the river was full and fast. "The currents are rapid and tricky," our guide Paloma told us. "We must keep to the inside on every turn. If we don't, the river will carry us into the tree branches, and if that happens, disobey your instincts. Do not duck! If you do, you will capsize. Use your paddle to push away from the branches."

We were intimidated, but the very muscular Tito joined us to paddle with Karen in a double. Adam and I were our own team. "There are crocodiles in this river," Paloma said, "but the crocs do not usually surface when the water is this fast. They should not attack a kayak."

Adam and I managed the first mile despite a few mild scrapes with branches and yelling at each other about steering right or left. Paloma observed our problems and mistook Adam as the source. He paired Adam with an experienced paddler and afterward he did fine, but I had more trouble without Adam than with him. The current swept me into low branches on the inside of a turn. When I panicked and frantically tried to back-paddle, Paloma yelled at me to push away with my paddle but old instincts kicked in and I hunched down. *Kaboom!* The boat capsized and I plummeted into the water. I could tell I feared capsizing more than the crocodiles because my heart stopped pounding as soon as I hit the water. I swam with desperate splashes to Paloma and Linda in their double. They towed me to the muddy shore, where Linda and I waited for him to return with help and she shared more of her life's turmoil.

Paloma and another guide, Ray, pulled up in two kayaks, and after much debate and gesturing they decided that I should swim and hold on to the strap at the back of Ray's single so he could paddle me back to the group. When we moved upstream, Ray asked me to kick to help him fight the current. I didn't mind the exercise since I was shivering. The group cheered when I arrived. I fished out and devoured a soggy P&J sandwich from my boat that had, by now, drifted to the landing.

I helped James and Linda into the motorboat with our kayaks piled horizontally on the stern. A mile downstream, I noticed that a Russian tourist seated across from me had raised and focused his camera. I looked in the direction of his lens and one of the largest crocodiles I had ever seen was stretched out on a log next to the muddy bank. The bank was identical to the one I'd just climbed onto. I said to the Russian guy, "That croc is fifteen feet long."

"No," he shouted, "About three meters."

Three meters or five meters, I was relieved that it was a mile away from my swim.

A nature walk was planned for late afternoon of the following day. Forewarned that the route was steep and muddy, we were fortified with shiny rubber wading boots. The path was not only muddy but also filled with puddles and crossed by overflowing streams, with boards serving as impromptu bridges occasionally strewn over slimy mud. The slippery downhill was worse than the uphill. I gave up my tedious, methodical descent and slid down the final two hundred feet on my muddy backside to be greeted by cheers and flashing cameras. We washed off the ooze and napped;

it was New Year's Eve and my family planned to stay awake until midnight.

Balloons and streamers decorated the dining room for a party that would begin right after dinner, but no one danced to the Latin music until James and Linda got things going. Linda gyrated her hips with gusto and shook her hands in the opposite direction while Jim moved with less enthusiasm but led her through her steps. Jim and Linda headed up a conga-line that snaked through the restaurant without faltering. Paloma held onto Linda and used the signals Rachel had taught him to keep the dancers from bumping into chairs or falling off the dance platform.

When the time neared, the hotel manager lined up fifty champagne glasses for a midnight toast. Suddenly fifty people materialized to celebrate with a *Feliz Nuevo Ano* clinking of glasses. The red-eyed tree frog that lived just outside the hotel pool hopped onto Adam's hand to wish him a happy new year.

We planned to raft out on New Year's Day, but the river was swollen and out of control. "We are at the mercy of nature. We will have to hike out," Paloma informed us. Our bags were packed into waterproof duffels and carried by extra workers from the lodge. The hike out was only an hour and a half in moderate mud. Our group finally reached the bus and everyone took off their shoes as we were told, but we barely drove twenty feet up the hill before backing down to let a car pass, and in the process the rear tires of the bus ground into the muddy road. We were stuck in a ditch! We evacuated the bus to lighten the load and walked shoeless up a rocky, mucky hill. Each time the driver pulled out, his wheels dug more deeply into the ooze. Our group huddled at the top of the hill until it started to rain, and we made our way back to the bus to stay dry and wait for help.

Over the next two and a half hours we asked several times when assistance would arrive and repeatedly heard the same answer: "Help will be here in a half hour." A four-cylinder jeep eventually showed up to pull the bus out while we pushed, but to no avail. Finally a rescue bus came and took us back to our hotel, a dozen mud-splattered hikers, two of them legally blind.

A year later, I jumped a curb just after nightfall and barely avoided an auto accident. Soon after this I was diagnosed with rapidly progressive cataracts in both eyes. I recalled my struggle to see in the dim twilight of the Costa Rican jungle. The spark of insight I'd had at that moment, that I was not so different from James and Linda, hit me again. Only a delicate surgical procedure protected me from becoming a traveler in the realm of the blind.

12

How Adam Coped With A Tibetan Trip At Ten

Tibet, China—Summer 2004

FRIENDS QUESTIONED WHY WE CHOSE Tibet and China as a family adventure trip, but Karen and I had our motives. She had a rapidly growing interest in Tibetan Buddhism and its connection to contemporary psychoanalysis. I looked forward to continuing my quest for a spiritual home amid the awe of a 12,000-foot-high civilization surrounded by mountain ranges towering over 28,000 feet.

We had left behind the formal trappings of our Catholicism and Judaism, although we had exposed Adam to both religions. Nevertheless, at ten he had already declared himself an agnostic. Taking Adam with us seemed a test, but we had traveled the world together and his global trips were already becoming an important part of his identity.

After waiting forty-one years for her first child, Karen was reluctant to be separated from him for two weeks. We were curious about how our Laguna Beach ten-year-old would respond to Tibet, not a typical destination for a child. Besides, there was no one to care for him except a family with a son who didn't surf, already an essential component of Adam's life.

We chose a tour that included five Tibetan cities: Tsedang, Chongye, Gyantse, Shigatse and Lhasa, as well as many rural monasteries.

Our plane emerged from the clouds, and the landscape of the Tibetan plateau unfolded before us: rugged, snow-covered mountains, tawny sand dunes, and rivers snaking their way through vertical canyons, irrigating rectangular barley farms. We landed and met our guide Tara, who delighted Adam by teasing him in her lilting Indian/British accent, "Today you rest, but in a few days I will work you like a slave." Her motions punctuated with melodious laughter, Tara placed white welcoming scarves around our necks. They had long strings like the *tallis* of Judaism.

Tara, just over five feet tall, had a strong mountain climber's body, essential for leading Himalayan treks. A striking mole poked out from the middle of her forehead, which she called her third eye, even if it was a bit off center.

We took on the mountain roads in a Land Cruiser that shook and rattled even on paved sections. The steering wheel vibrated like a tuning fork, and the gearshift was attached to the four-wheel drive shaft by a rubber band. The broken front door handle dangled on the passenger's side of the car, its loose rusty screw pointing inward, an inch from my arm.

Tsedang

Our group stayed at the Tsedang Hotel, the most luxurious in the city of the same name, although this Chinese-built structure was without character. Karen was feeling queasy but came with us on our first adventure to the Tibetan part of town, nestled against the mountain and far more charming than the Chinese section, with doors of red lacquer and gold leaf surrounded by geometric patterns and swirling dragons.

I startled an elderly man when I quickly came around a curve, though his demeanor shifted from alarm to a welcoming smile. I wondered if the Tibetan gentleness I observed everywhere was a result of Buddhist compassion and kindness or joy at seeing tourists again.

Adam adjusted his camera to capture water being lobbed in a mock battle among gleeful Tibetan youth in a monastery courtyard. Karen was by now too sick from acute mountain sickness to climb up to the monastery, so Adam and I scaled the stairs with Tara. Karen's health was beginning to concern me, but I expected she'd recover in a day or two, just like at Mammoth Mountain back home, and scamper ahead of me.

Adam and I returned to the room to find Karen between a light doze and agonizing nausea. Tara brought biscuits and Rhodiola capsules, which relieved her symptoms so she could sleep through the night. Karen was hoping she'd get better soon, but I was getting worried because she'd never reacted to altitude with this much retching. Karen joined the group for a breakfast of toast and special tea the next morning. She waited in the temple with Tara while Adam and I ascended to the top of the hill for a view of a sea of gray cement roofs. Several Tibetan Pilgrims touched fair-skinned blond Adam on the way up to bring themselves good fortune, but he was even more caressed by their smiling dark eyes. Upon descending, the loud clattering of yaks, horses, and donkeys startled us as they tore up the hill carrying Japanese tourists, then raced back down to pick up the rest of the busload that had just arrived. The frenzy to get the tour group up to the top turned the gentle Tibetan horsemen into New York City cabbies.

Chongye

A teenage Chinese boy tentatively approached our family shortly after we arrived at Chongye. He was dressed neatly in a crew-neck sweater vest with a plaid shirt, his sleeves impeccably folded three inches above his wrist, dark hair perfectly cut in bangs falling just above his eyebrows. He introduced himself in a child-like voice: "Excuse me, my parents say I should talk to you to practice my English. My name is Wentzi. It means mosquito." Who names their kid after an insect, I wondered, especially a kid who seems more obedient than pesky.

Adam hesitated until I urged him to tell Wentzi his name, "My name is Adam. I come from Laguna Beach, California, America."

"I am starting middle school in Hunan, China."

Adam said, "I am starting fifth grade in California."

I told Wentzi I thought he spoke English rather well, and he replied, "I do not speak well English. My English teacher speaks very well English."

Searching for a point of contact, Adam informed Wentzi that he lived near Disneyland—no connection. I asked if he knew about Yao Ming, the international basketball star —again, no connection. Wentzi's mother and father moved closer to him and murmured a suggestion in his ear.

Wentzi responded, "This is the first time I have been abroad." I found 'abroad' an interesting word choice, since the government of China considers any attempt to regard Tibet as a separate country a security threat. I assumed it was merely a quirk of vocabulary. The fifteen-year-old Wentzi took Adam's hand in his and they posed for several pictures taken by both proud families. Wentzi forced a happy smile while Adam removed his hat and revealed his disheveled blonde hair. Wentzi took off his silver *om* necklace and gave it to Adam, who reciprocated with a gift of his Death Valley Junior Ranger pin. For the moment, our children had bridged a massive cultural gap.

Samye

The boat to Samye monastery was primitively fashioned of rotting wood and overflowing with pilgrims. It looked as if it could sink at any moment. Two men on the shore launched it into the water with planks of wood. The women wore brightly colored beads over even brighter multi-patterned clothing. The medley included red-rose imprinted blouses, iridescent fuchsia scarves, plaid kerchiefs, and waist-length hair braided with purple, green, and white cloth. A bald monk sat at the bow, unflustered by the crowds.

Nine tractors greeted the boat and carted the locals up to the monastery, while our group packed onto a red and gray bus. Adam experimented further with his camera, lying on the ground or asking people to step aside to improve his shots, using photography to combat the boredom of an adult-oriented journey.

I climbed to the top of the central temple and looked down onto the mandala arrangement of structures surrounding me. Adam had an idea that there was "a nice place called enlightenment" at the top, but neither of us found it there. Still, I found it peaceful to be surrounded by a three-dimensional replica of the Tibetan Buddhist universe at the peak of this ancient monastery.

Monks chanted prayers chosen from thousands of ancient scrolls stored against the wall. The chants reminded me of prayers of Orthodox Jews I'd heard long ago. A monk slowly banged a huge drum with a stick that had a pair of cymbals attached to it, the metallic beat helping maintain the rhythm of the chant.

Returning to the boat, our bus passed several tractors packed with Tibetans and honked the smaller vehicles to the side, yet the pilgrims managed to fill the boat before we even tried to board. Tara persuaded them to make room and they quickly cleared a place for my family. The Tibetans took us by the hand, guiding us over the high benches to our seats. Just when we thought the boat was filled to overflowing, a bus packed with Japanese tourists emptied, and each of them squeezed into a previously nonexistent spot. The Tibetans continued to show their warm and generous character, giving up their seats, posing for pictures, touching Adam gently and smiling toothless smiles.

We left the boat by walking on the same plank used to pull the craft onto the pebbly shore, where Land Cruisers waited to take us to Lhasa for a brief overnight. On the roadside, three naked boys partially covered with mud and about Adam's age jumped up and down and gleefully waved to us. We came to a stop at a checkpoint staffed by Chinese police as we approached the road to the airport. The policewoman who checked our driver's papers spoke to him sharply and angrily jerked his identification out of his hand. I wasn't frightened by this angry Chinese presence; I experienced it as more posturing than threatening.

We took the northern road to Gyantse since the shorter southern route was closed for repairs. The drive took ten hours on bumpy, curvy mountain roads. I was never bored, surrounded by 22,000-foot-high jagged mountains and holding on to the ceiling strap while cars, their horns blasting, passed slower vehicles on blind curves. We were told our driver, Bamba, was one of the safest drivers on the road. My heart pounded when the car stalled on steep grades, and I remembered I didn't have a seat belt. Our car stalled often, and each time Bamba lifted the hood, removed the carburetor, blew mightily into it, replaced it and we would take off again. The yaks, sheep, cows, and goats provided entertainment while we drove at altitudes higher than I'd ever been. Yaks and cows interbreed, producing a hybrid called a *dzo*, so it is difficult at times to tell them apart. Even the goats have whiskers and horns that point up and out, just like the yaks.

Our route took us over a high pass of 16,500 feet. Karen had stopped suffering from altitude sickness and was coping with the elevation quite well by now. Soft snow surrounded us when we reached the high point of our climb.

How Adam Coped with a Tibetan Trip at Ten

We pulled over to celebrate among well-dressed Italian tourists streaming out of their buses and vendors selling prayer flags. Karen purchased several sets of the long strips of red, white, blue, yellow, and green flags for our yard in California. Adam and I tried to have a snowball fight, but the dry snow didn't stick. We all laughed triumphantly at being on the highest ground of our lives, but we moved sluggishly.

Our car stalled in front of a nomad summer festival and we pulled over to have Bamba once again blow out the carburetor. Dozens of children ran toward us as Karen coaxed Adam out to greet them. He was mobbed by the kids as if he were a movie star or perhaps because he was a rarely, if ever seen, blonde boy dressed like a Gap model with safari clothing and yellow Tibetan neck scarf.

A truck that was only a few minutes ahead of us had plunged over an embankment and dropped 50 feet, smashing the driver's cab. No one was hurt, but the driver was distraught and pacing. In a country without insurance, his life savings were lost. This was the second truck we had seen overturned by the side of the road. The battered trucks left me frightened about the rest of the drive. What if the driving skills we so admired were not enough to overcome the risk of passing on blind curves?

I asked Adam how he had managed the ten-hour drive without seeming bored or impatient. "When we drove along the river I imagined I was a river guide and how I would lead the boats through the water," he said. "I love driving off road. The bumpiness is like being on a roller coaster." He volunteered that he had listened to his portable CD player for about an hour, and he ate some sweet candy he'd brought from home.

Shigatse

Tara negotiated a Tibetan-style suite with antique rugs and purple and green neon-hued pillows for us in Shigatse. At dinner Adam asked Tara what had happened to the Panchen Lama who was chosen by the Dalai Lama. "Is he still in prison? Is he still alive?" Tara whispered back, "Talk about that in private, not in hotel dining rooms." She then announced in her normal voice to any lurking eavesdroppers, "He's a child. He doesn't know what he's asking."

We drove from there to Tashilhunpo Monastery, the site of Asia's largest bronze Buddha, where the monks put their arms around Adam and gave him a prayer shawl to go with his prayer necklace and bracelet. Adam occupied himself during our many visits to monasteries by having his beads blessed by every Buddha we approached. He pressed the tips of his fingers to his forehead and bowed, then rubbed the beads between his hands before the Buddha. Adam loved taking pictures of the monks inside the monasteries as well as the many dogs that congregated outside, laughing when he learned they were reincarnations of recalcitrant monks.

Our car had been in the shop for a day and was to have been in top shape for the drive back to Lhasa. I fastened the seat belt, and Bamba laughed at me. It was extremely uncomfortable to wear and bit into my shoulder, but since I had requested that it be fixed, I wore it the entire way back. The door, windows, and handles had been securely fastened with duct-tape, and the screws were now covered, but the engine wouldn't start. Bamba found a rock by the road, opened the hood and tapped the engine a few times—at least he didn't blow out the carburetor. He returned to the car, started the engine with one turn of the key and smiled at us, a routine he would repeat when the car stalled. Somehow he knew when to bang the engine and when to huff the carburetor.

When we returned to the top of the mountain pass, the three of us bounded out of the car, scampered up to the summit, threw snow in the air, embraced and screamed with joy. We had our energy back and the reverberating void of the 16,500-foot peak all to ourselves. Mutual exuberance at a shared accomplishment brought a feeling of instant closeness. The high of such a connection is one reason we go on so many adventure trips.

Lhasa

I stepped out of my hotel in Lhasa and found myself on a pilgrimage circuit around the important monasteries of the city. Many pilgrims walked briskly by me, twirling their prayer wheels and chanting; others stepped meditatively, synchronizing their breath with their pace.

The hotel is only two blocks from the Barkhor bazaar, one of the largest open markets I've ever seen. Seven-foot-high incense burners filled the square with the powerful smoke of burning leaf-laden twigs of juniper. The Barkhor bustled with vendors, shoppers, and pilgrims. Businesses and shops lined the streets and alleys around the circuit. Surveillance cameras looked down upon us, closely monitored by Chinese observers fearful of rebellions starting in the marketplace. Open-air booths, stalls, and pushcarts were everywhere, packed with everything from baseball caps and luggage to pots and pans. In the narrow streets roving hustlers sold pirated music cassettes and prayer wheels, brushing by prostrating pilgrims exhaling heavily as they slid across the stone pavement worn smooth. Adam bargained for, then swung, a prayer wheel as he made his way through the market.

Thousands of Tibetans lined up to enter the Jokhang, slowly slithering their way into the temple to worship the great golden Sakyamuni Buddha. Tara and Adam snuck under the restraining wire and bowed before the statue of the Buddha. The rancid milky odor of burning yak butter emanated from candleholders inside the doorway.

Adam spotted a group of young people singing, dancing, and pounding a roof into place with round cement stompers attached to a wooden pole. He joined them and figured out how a lefty can stamp and circle clockwise, though he never quite got the song. The magnificent Potala Palace loomed over the other side of the roof, a thirteen-level red and white storybook castle built on a massive solid rock.

We passed a courtyard at the entrance to the Sera Monastery, one day before the ceremony of unfurling an enormous Buddha tapestry. There we heard a loud hum of voices punctuated by snapping and clapping sounds. "That's the monks debating," Tara said, "but let's first go into the great hall."

Our group met five Tibetan women near the entrance. The oldest told us she was seventy-two and introduced her younger sister and three friends. Each of them wore a multi-striped, seemingly bar code-patterned apron of different shades, so no color was repeated. The women wore gray vests with iridescent blouses of chartreuse and fuchsia. Three had turbans, which matched the blouses perfectly, and two had their hair braided with bright ribbons. Their smiles, though toothless, radiated friendliness and when I took the hand of the eldest, she didn't let go. All the pilgrims laughed at our clasped hands and my inability or unwillingness to get free.

Karen asked us to hurry into the courtyard where the monks' debate was taking place. They clapped their hands together to emphasize arguments during the debate, the sound as sharp and loud as caps and fireworks I've heard during Chinese New Year's celebrations. Some 200 monks in crimson robes were gathered in small groups debating questions such as What is the mind? The voice? Water? Dharma? One monk lunged forward in a graceful Tae Kwon Do-like movement and slapped his hands in affirmation of his point, as if to say, "So what do you think about that?" I wanted to ask, "What is awareness like in the afterlife?" Most of the monks were laughing, teasing, and smiling until their teacher came over to evaluate them and then they suddenly became very serious.

Several novitiates beckoned Adam to join them and laughed when he moved into their group. Each time Adam left a monk's side, the entire circle waved their cupped hands beckoning Adam to come back in. When Adam held back, they gently tossed pebbles next to him to get his attention.

The monks chanted in rhythm, faster and faster, until the notes became a whirling hum. Even during the chant they kept clowning around and waving and whistling to Adam to join them. The head lama blessed Adam's beads as my son bowed before him, then took Adam's hands in his and clasped them firmly. I was surprised to see the lama was wearing high-topped hiking boots below his crimson robe.

Our last day in Tibet was the only cloudy day of our stay and it rained when we reached Norbulingka, the former palace of the Dalai Lama. Drops of rain on the tips of leaves lining our path shone like pearls in the mist. Brightly colored banners hung from the high ceiling of the great hall. Underneath the banners sat dozens of monks folding prayer flags. Adam was interested to learn that the Dalai Lama had kept a bedroom for his mother in a section of his quarters and I was certain Adam would like to do the same. I felt the Dalai Lama's presence more than at any other place in Tibet; here, in his former home and amid his furniture, I was saddened when I realized he could not return to his country.

We emerged from the palace and returned to grounds packed with elaborate embroidered tents, all soaked through and dripping water inside and out. Thousands of locals crowded in front of an open-air stage where traditional Chinese opera is performed. Adam, perched on my shoulders, was the only one of us who could view any part of the performance. The Chinese opera was screechy and unappealing in the rain. We made our way out of the palace grounds through many rare plants from all over the world donated to the Dalai Lama throughout the centuries. As we exited, the Chinese music blasting from a loud speaker suddenly changed to Brittany Spears singing, "Hit Me Baby, One More Time."

The tour group returned to a rug factory owned by Tara's brother for a traditional Tibetan farewell dinner. A multitude of local staples were served, including bland yak cheese, *tsampa* or roasted barley flower, and thick yak meat that tastes like pork when thick and roast beef when sliced thin, according to Adam. He also tried the famous yak milk tea but, unable to tolerate the tiniest sip, Adam let the thick liquid slide out of his mouth in a continuous spaghetti-like line down to the tabletop. Karen and I put down our cups of yak milk tea and picked up our first glass of wine on this trip.

We went outside between courses and joined the factory workers and dozens of neighbors in a circular folk dance. An eight-year-old boy took Adam by the hand and led him to a playground outside the walls of the factory where they played together. Adam's first opportunity to dance and play with children had waited until the last moments of our Tibetan trip. He was getting restless, even though he had seemed to adapt through using his imagination, camera, and prayer beads. After our farewell dinner he sang us a song in his hoarse but melodious voice:

> I miss my friends. I'm getting bored,
> I've been to a monastery every single day,
> I'm tired of adult conversations at dinner,
> I don't want to sit through another adult conversation

Tara gave each of us a gift of hand-made parchment cards, a yellow shawl, and prayer flags. She wrote a personal note to our family: "Thank you for your wonderful company on this Tibet trip. It has been a lot of fun for me to have Adam on this trip. People loved him everywhere we went."

Beijing

The city of Beijing was a marked contrast to Tibet and had modernized since my last trip there in the late 1970s. It was now a thriving metropolis and our hotel, the Sheraton Great Wall, was as elegant as we'd want it to be. We toured without a guide and could go anywhere in the city as long as we had a hotel card with directions written in Chinese to help us find our way back.

As we walked the streets of Beijing, Adam twirled his camera by the strap as he often does. We turned toward a taxi stand when his eyes met those of a man dressed in black who brushed up against him. Adam heard a quick zip. He lifted up his digital camera case and saw that his camera was no longer in it. Speedy Adam ran into the crowd to try to find the thief while Karen and I trailed behind. When we caught up, he was crying.

Karen remarked, "This wouldn't have happened in Tibet where people went out of their way to return things we'd left behind." Adam was angry with himself for not grabbing the thief and demanding the camera back. "I want to give him the finger," Adam said, then his anger shifted. "I want to go home. I hate China. I hope they lose every Olympic event."

The morning after the theft, Adam with camcorder in hand, Karen with her digital camera, and I, with pad and pencil, made our way to the Forbidden City. This huge complex of red-walled buildings and pavilions, roofed by glazed vermillion tile, contains what is said to be 9,999 rooms. The Chinese love the number nine, and the emperor who built it could not exceed the 10,000-room palace of his father without threat of inevitable misfortune. The only commercial store in the palace was Starbucks, amazingly, for the Forbidden City was a place where, not long ago, any foreigner who entered could be executed. A few years later I would learn to my great relief that the Starbucks had been removed.

I looked forward to our last day since it involved a visit to the Great Wall, high up on my bucket list. We chose the Simitai section of the wall, a three-hour drive from our hotel and difficult to reach by public transportation. The choice was easy for me since the guidebooks describe Simitai as spectacularly beautiful and peaceful.

Badaling, the section of the wall most often visited because it is closer to Beijing, is incredibly crowded. The Great Wall at Simitai is built on steep mountainous slopes so it rises and falls more sharply than other sections of the wall. It also is harder to climb. A set of two trams took us to a point only 150 feet below a lower part of the wall we could climb more easily. Parts of Simitai are so steep and dangerous they were closed off after several deaths occurred.

The Great Wall, one of the Seven Wonders of the World, was the reason I had chosen to spend time in Beijing. As an old Chinese saying goes, "You are not a man unless you have been to The Great Wall." The wall, if stretched out, would measure 3,000 miles, but it zigzags so much along mountain ridges that it covers only half that distance. It was first built in the seventh century B.C. and when sections of it were brought together in the second century B.C., a million people or one-fifth of the work force of the country was required to work on its construction. Many of the laborers died agonizing deaths.

The drive through the countryside on our way home was refreshing. Tall corn, ripe pumpkins, and giant squash grew in abundance. Fresh fruit stands were omnipresent, selling shiny apples, peaches, and plums. This rural part of China has a peaceful, natural beauty and the people we met here live life at a slower pace than in Beijing. They seemed less focused on money and interested in nature's beauty, much like the Tibetans we had just left.

Adam's newly acquired photography skills, adaptability, and creativity helped him survive and even enjoy our spiritual pilgrimage. His journey prepared him for challenging adventures yet to come. Karen was convinced she would study Buddhism more extensively. I had found my Shangri-La and experienced a peacefulness that gave me hints of answers to questions I was starting to ask myself.

13

Tibetan Brotherhood

Tibet, Summer 2004

Pilgrims crane their necks and gaze at the unfurling of the one hundred-foot-long tapestry of the Buddha, their craggy faces carved by years of mountain winds.

Four eight-foot brass horns jut out over the top of the tongka. Young monks blow these elongated horns in unison, producing a sound deeper than the croak of a bullfrog. A miniature instrument emits a high-pitched, tinny bagpipe sound that alternates with the deep bass. After an hour, the thick pungent odor and smoke of juniper incense recedes so I can breathe and see the Buddha across the courtyard.

I find myself spontaneously chanting a Hebrew prayer I had learned fifty years ago and rarely sung since. *Henay matov oh ma nayim. Shevat ahim gam yah had.*

An Israeli friend later reminds me this was a Sabbath prayer that translates to "How good it is to be with the twelve tribes or brothers of Israel." When I learned its meaning, I realized that for a brief moment in Tibet I had experienced a brotherhood with the Tibetan people.

We had tried to leave by the same side of the temple that we'd entered, but hundreds of pilgrims were streaming toward us and two policemen stopped us from walking in that direction. Our guide, Tara, caught a sympathetic look in the eye of another policeman and told him that we had several sick "*cheekas*" (Tibetan slang for Caucasians) on the other side of the hill and must reach them as soon as possible. She emphasized her point with a loud clap of her hands and said, "How could I tell a lie here under the eye of God?"

The officer motioned us down the path, but every pilgrim we passed pointed us back the other way. About halfway down we stopped and Tara led us in a choral rendition of *Om Mani Padme Hum*. We sat in our best Lotus position and held our hands with thumb and forefinger shaped in an *om*. I sang with my usual off-key gusto, maintaining my awareness that six *cheekas* were quite a strange sight chanting together on the hill leading to the ancient monastery of Sera. The pilgrims were delighted by our performance, bowing and beaming in approval as they passed.

An elderly white-bearded Tibetan man stopped and we greeted each other. I asked Tara to tell him I thought he was handsome. He looked deeply into my eyes and I struggled to return the contact, so deep was his gaze. He responded by tweaking my beard and I pulled his in return, reaching out to him as best I could. He squeezed my hand for what seemed forever. Our eyes met again. This time I let myself feel his compassion.

I think about how often I have felt close to my fellow elders in foreign lands, despite my inability to speak their language. I felt his love not just for me but also for humanity. Still, I wondered if I were a victim of a common syndrome in which foreigners attribute great wisdom to every Tibetan they meet.

14

On Our Own In Alaska

Uganik Bay, Summer 2004

Adam and I flew from Anchorage to Kodiak Island. From there we took a four-seater floatplane to visit my friend Toby in Uganik Bay. The island was sculpted into green fjords, spiny peaks, and curved bays that zigzagged so no point of land was farther than fifteen miles from the ocean.

Toby's beach was too rocky for the plane's pontoons so we landed on the other side of the point and Toby motored out in his skiff to pick us up. Toby's twelve-year-old son, Abraham, met us as soon as we got out of the boat. He gave Adam an Alaskan version of a hipster's handshake—clasping hands, touching fists, rubbing elbows—which Adam struggled to return. Toby introduced us to his daughter, Jordan, his teenage nephews, Colin and Alek, and his youthful crew, Corey and Jacob.

Toby is a salmon fisherman and a writer. He is about my height at 5-foot-11 but seems taller. He has ruddy Irish good looks with long, graying curly hair and a black pearl stud in his left ear. Bushy eyebrows frame drooping upper eyelids that drop down over the outer parts of his eyes and create creases extending out an inch from both lids. The sagging lids give his glaucous blue eyes a permanent squint.

His property consists of a cabin with two bedrooms, a sleeping loft with ample windows that overlook the harbor and sunsets, a yurt-shaped tent, and an outhouse. The main house is elevated on top of a small bluff, about fifteen feet higher than the sandy beach. The structures are surrounded by Alaskan irises, purple columbine, violet lupin, chocolate lilies that smelled like baby's diapers, yaro, watermelon berries and the dreaded pushki. Adam was afraid of pushki because Colin and Abe told him if it touched his skin, a terrible rash would overwhelm him.

The side-yard is typically rural Alaskan in that it features several rusted fuel drums, which have been euphemistically termed "the national flower of Alaska" since they are so common and necessary, yet difficult to get rid of. The rest of the yard was cluttered with a bathtub, ropes, buoys, a rusted anchor, a ladder, two outboard motors, and a clothes washer. Three-foot-high beach grass was growing everywhere, even spouting from the drain of the abandoned tub.

At 10:30 a.m. the sun shone brightly so it seemed natural to sit down for dinner at that time. Karen had urged me to try to get Adam to sleep close to his usual time of 9 p.m., but the height of the sun and the biological rhythm of the camp made it impossible. Adam ran around the waterfront property and swung on the hammock with the other boys after dinner so we didn't settle into our loft sleeping space until after midnight.

The sun rose from perpetual twilight at 4:15 our first morning. We awakened a few hours later to blazing light and warm temperatures. Adam, Toby, and I set out in Toby's skiff to bottom-fish. Toby took us to his secret spot for halibut and we let our hand lines down 180 fathoms (30 feet). I wondered how I could reel in one of the famous local one hundred-pound halibut with a hand line. Adam chose a rod and bottom-fished with a shiny metal lure and screamed, "Oh yeah, oh yeah" when he reeled in a one-pound rock bass.

For lunch Adam munched on bass, while the rest of us had salmon since we caught no halibut. I also had salmon for dinner that day and I wondered how many more meals of fresh salmon I could handle. By the end of our stay we'd had salmon curry, salmon tacos, salmon with rice and black beans, salmon linguine, salmon salad, and cold salmon sandwiches with diced mango.

In previous summers, I was told, when blackberries and salmonberries were ripe and plentiful, bears feasted by the cabin and even broke down the back door. I saw deep paw marks as evidence. When Toby went to the back of the cabin to fix a water line, he brought along a gun proclaiming "It's bear country back that way."

Toby told us with a scowl of disgust about neighbors less than a mile down the bay who were feeding the carcasses of huge halibut to the bears and taking pictures of them. I was hoping to see the bears eat the salmon heads and tails we'd left for eagles on our beach but they were content with the neighbors' halibut.

This trip was the longest period of time Adam and his mother had ever been apart. By the third night, Adam was having trouble sleeping, even though his mattress was right next to mine in the narrow low-ceilinged loft. He brought his sleeping bag closer to mine, cuddled up and soon fell asleep. He was really missing his mother and the next morning demanded we call her.

"Dad, you promised I could talk to mom today!" he pleaded.

Toby told me at breakfast that the Coast Guard had called the cannery with a message from Karen. She wanted to know why we hadn't called her and if we were having problems. Toby didn't want to tell us about this until he could figure out a way to call. Toby, Adam, and I boated to the house of his friend Lisa, who reassured Adam that she had an Internet phone connection. Adam and I climbed to the second floor where Lisa taught Adam how to use the

Internet phone, which had an eight-second delay, making it challenging to use. She set it up for Adam to use on speakerphone and after he said "hello" there was a pause until Karen's voice finally reverberated loudly through the house, "Adammmmmm."

Lisa's pet dog, too small to be a musher, lived in her cabin with her. "Who wants to pull a sled?" she asked, and the little dog raised its right paw and jumped up and down. It danced on command, spinning and hopping in a circle with its paws curled upwards.

Our first day on the boat Toby and Corey left Adam and me on the holding skiff while they delivered salmon to a larger boat called a tender. The tender can store up to 200,000 pounds of iced fish. The holding skiff was a twenty-foot-long dinghy with several metal chests of ice in which salmon had been sorted and stored until the fish could be delivered to the tender. Adam and I were dressed in borrowed rubber pants, jackets, boots, and life vests. Toby and Corey invited us into their boat to see the catch that had been trapped in the net since the last pick, just four hours before this one.

"Keep your hands inside when climbing over from your boat to ours," Corey warned us. "The waves can suddenly jerk the edges of the boats in opposite directions and can chop your fingers in a split second."

Toby and Corey set up two pairs of steel rods a foot

apart at either end of the boat and placed the net through the rods. As the net passed through the slowly moving boat, we first saw kelp, then a few pieces of jelly-fish, and suddenly a ten-pound red salmon appeared. Adam and I would've loved to catch this large, stunning fish with rod and reel, given the one-pounders we'd been catching. We were considered "green guys" and were not much help with the net despite our authentic outfits. The yield that day was a disappointing 350 pounds. A good catch can yield several thousand, but Adam and I were amazed by the amount of salmon we saw popping up among the kelp and the masses of jellyfish. The silver or coho were just starting to come in and Toby saved a few for dinner and threw the rest back in the bay. Toby's salmon income had dropped to about a third of what it was a few years ago because of competition from farmed salmon.

The tender, owned and operated by the cannery, is the umbilical cord of the fish camp since it brings groceries, mail, and Federal Express packages. It weighs the fish and transports them back to the cannery. The tender did not have our long-awaited food order, but it did bring a copy of the *Anchorage Press*, which everyone devoured when we returned to the cabin. Each time Toby delivered a load of fish, the tender operator gave him a gift as an incentive to bring the freshest fish possible. This time the reward was a six-pack of generic soda and a quart of ice cream.

After a few days, the blistering heat left and the weather changed to a typical Uganik summer, cool and cloudy with choppy seas. The shift in the weather brought poor sport fishing but Adam wanted to try it. He snagged his line into a rat's nest and couldn't cast. I asked him if he wanted help and he replied, "Dad, let me do one thing myself." He solved the problem himself and returned to fishing. I was aware of the dance between us as we alternately leaned forward and bobbed back when we cast, snapped, and reeled in our lines.

Colin and Alek didn't seem able to dent my confident son's equanimity with their criticisms so they intensified their name-calling and resorted to calling him "Shitty Boy." He bit his lip, came to me and cried when he told me what they'd called him. I held him close and told him they were bad for being so nasty. I wished that Abraham's cousins hadn't come because when they weren't around, Adam and Abraham got along famously. One day Adam and Abe wrestled playfully like two bear cubs for almost an hour in the grass. Thirteen-year-old Alek arose from his usually recumbent position to watch their play then wisecracked, "It looks like they're groping each other." Later that day, Colin and Alek threw Adam out of their yurt-shaped tent onto a pile of laundry, which left Adam on the verge of tears until they kicked Abe out too.

Stormy weather drove the boys inside for chess and Scrabble. Suddenly I heard Adam and Abraham shouting,

"The boat is sinking! The boat is sinking!" Colin and Jacob accused the younger boys of joking, until they looked out the window and saw the skiff rapidly filling up with water. Suddenly the cabin emptied out before the swinging door could shut. Toby grabbed his waterproof gear as he angrily shouted to me, "They sunk my boat!" When I arrived, its contents were bobbing next to shore and the kids were hopping on the rocks to retrieve the equipment: oars, radio, life vests, GPS, storage boxes, and a few cans of generic soda. Jake, clad only in a T-shirt and shorts, was furiously bailing out the boat. The motor and new radio were soaked and useless.

Toby and Corey worked on the motor for hours and got it working perfectly, but the radio was a loss. Three other fishermen working nearby called and offered to help fix equipment or pick the net. Toby turned down their help because, as he said, "It's the independent Alaskan way, and we like to do things ourselves. Besides Uganik is a haven for control freaks."

I interjected, "People help each other out."

"Yeah," Toby continued, "but the ethic is to do it yourself and not ask for help."

That night, after we climbed up to our sleeping loft, Adam said he felt a little like throwing up, which he did on occasion when he missed his mother. He moved his sleeping bag over to my mattress and immediately fell asleep.

We had the opportunity to take an early flight from Uganik to Kodiak on our way back home and, if we made it, to see bears in nearby Katmai Peninsula. We needed to leave by 9:30 a.m. to catch this flight, though. The fog was rolling in and if we missed the early flight the afternoon plane may never take off. Toby said," I can't leave till the tender comes. We've got a full load of fish and I have no room for the next pick." At 9:45 he said, "No word from the tender, so I'll take you to the plane and hope I make it back in time."

We tore away from the shore and said our goodbyes only to a family of bald eagles, as everyone in the cabin was still asleep. The 10:15 Horizon Airways float plane flew over us at 10:12 and landed just beyond us on the other side of a peninsula. We reached the plane just as it was taxiing away from the beach. We waved, jumped up and down, and lifted two fingers to indicate we were two passengers. The pilot did not respond to Toby's attempt to contact him on his radio; he waved goodbye and made what looked like a peace sign back to us.

We climbed off the boat at a house belonging to Dave and Linda, whose flat sandy beach was the scheduled plane stop. They invited us in for coffee and juice while we waited for the plane. Dave was bald with a rim of white beard and a sweet glowing grin that caressed his otherwise expressionless face. Linda had dyed red hair in a five-inch upsweep and wore an orthopedic cervical collar. They had the largest personal collection of videos I had ever seen, including over fifty John Wayne movies. Dave, who around this time was working on the water pump under the house, said he had seen balls of spiders up to two feet in circumference, each ball containing thousands of spiders clustered together. Linda said the balls reminded her of King Crabs she had seen.

"I saw a ball of crabs, big as the living room," she says.

Dave responded with, "I saw a ball of crabs as big as this house."

"We had balls of Daddy Longlegs in this attic," Linda countered. "They have a real rank odor like stink bugs. I climbed up there once and pushed them away, but they rolled back on me and stunk. I went down, got the bug spray and made a mistake I'll never make again—I sprayed them. The ball of bugs broke up and Daddy Longlegs kept dropping through the ceiling half dead for days."

Linda hovered over the radio. The weather channel had just broadcast the visibility as zero. "Pay no mind," Linda said, "you're on island time now and you just take things as they come." I tried to accept my powerlessness but it was hard. At home I get anxious if traffic slows a bit on the way to LAX.

By now it was noon and no word from either plane, so I bothered Linda to try and contact the dispatchers but she said, "Phone calls are expensive." She brought out a lunch of peanut butter and jelly and, of course, salmon salad. Adam had a sandwich of each.

We never did hear from Dean, the Horizon pilot who waved goodbye to us with a peace sign, but at 2:15 our pilot Jaime from Island Air called to say that he would be landing in twenty minutes. I borrowed binoculars and scoured the beach on the other side of the island for one last chance to see the bears I'd heard were there that morning. The plane swooped down between two rock outcroppings and suddenly appeared as Adam snapped its trail of ocean spray. We were so relieved to see the plane that we greeted Jaime with cheers and warm handclasps on the verge of hugs. I put on the earphones and mike and felt like a copilot in the front seat while Adam sat right behind me, shooting pictures with his digital.

The green tundra-like moss below us took on an even deeper beauty now that we had experienced its many trees, flowers and grasses. Here, the high tide turns hundreds of peninsulas into tiny islands. The ocean spills over rocky walls and forms frothy lakes. As we rose above craggy peaks, below us we saw crystalline pools of melted snow. We dipped down out of the fog and Jaime skillfully landed the plane and taxied to the unloading dock.

We woke the next morning to a fog that didn't appear to be lifting and knew that at times the fog can prevent all planes from taking off and landing for days. Everyone in the waiting area of the airport was discussing the fog; the ceiling was right on the cusp of landability. Adam and I watched the runway for signs of our flight. Then the plane broke through the fog and taxied in, right in front of the window we were facing.

Once on board, Adam and I sat next to each other and wrote in our journals, though I could hardly move my arm to write as he snuggled next to me. If his mother had been there, he'd have been scrunched up with her instead. With Karen out of the picture, I had eased up on him—driven him less to write, do chores or read, yet he did all these reasonably well on his own, particularly if I counted surfing magazines. This time he only had me to cuddle with at night and his alienation from the older boys had driven him even closer to me, perhaps the closest we'd ever been.

15

Stirring in Sayulita

Mexico, Winter 2006

It is festival time in Sayulita, Mexico, a sleepy-about-to-awaken-fishing village forty minutes north of Puerto Vallarta. The carnival celebration takes up a square block by the ocean and is bordered by the effluent river that the town is actively trying to purify.

The rich odor of burnt buttered popcorn mixes with the stench of the fetid stream. Adam, Eric, and Paul, seventh graders at Thurston Middle School in Laguna Beach, head for a ride called the Himalaya. A virtually nude, large-breasted woman in high heels is painted on the wall in back of them. The cars circle forward to load new passengers, leaving the boys behind the wall and out of sight for several minutes. Karen expresses concern about what could happen to them back there. Finally the ride starts and the boys come back into view. The car spins the boys around and builds up speed then suddenly reverses direction and moves backward, squishing them into each other. The scratchy music grows louder and louder, a thumping Mariachi Techno. The ride goes on and on, well worth the twenty-peso admission.

The boys have run out of money so they choose a two-story Jolly Jumper, the only free ride at the fiesta. They climb to the top level, steadily bounce up to the ceiling and throw a large inflated multi-colored ball back and forth. Suddenly, two more balls squeeze into the trampoline area heralding the arrival of three athletic, local Mexican girls, about a year younger than the boys. All six spring faster and higher in unison, throwing the balls harder and stronger except for Adam, whose dodge ball expertise has always been at ducking and not throwing.

The girls' squeals of delight intensify, their throws become more forceful, their screams even louder when they dropkick the balls at the boys. Eric easily catches the hard shots; he is the goalie on the Laguna Beach Junior Olympic Water Polo team. Adam jumps on two balls and rolls over on his back in a comic attempt at a relaxed pose. The girls grab the balls from him and pull them away. Adam bounces to the floor. He jumps up, tries to seize a ball back, but the girls hold tight. They toss it at him, now gently and with giggles; their throws became lighter and laughter more tender. The girls' eyelids simultaneously drop and flutter seductively just as the battle ends. They all exit the bounce house and Eric approaches the girls shouting, "*Soy ganadores.*"

Eric translates this as "We won."

My thought, one I knew the boys were not even close to accepting, was that the victory was not how well they played ball, but how unknowingly they and the girls had simmered into the passions of the game together.

16

Eddie Spaghetti

Philadelphia—1945, 2010

MY PARENTS, SISTER, AND I LIVED in South Philadelphia with my aunt and grandmother in a small row house until I was nine. The house was a few doors away from Seventh Street, lined with teeming pushcarts piled high with discount clothing, fresh vegetables, kosher meat, and fish on ice sold by hawkers with thick Yiddish accents.

My grandmother took in a newly immigrated Italian man named Rocco, who lived as a boarder in our third floor garret. Bubba put up her long gray hair in a tightly curled braid held together by a bleached tortoise shell comb. Roccov, as she called him, taught her how to make spaghetti. In her world everyone had a Jewish name, even Ed Solomon's (Ed Sullivan's) variety show. I loved her pasta and ate so much of it I was called Eddie Spaghetti. My mother was a mediocre cook, but by the time we moved out of my grandmother's house she could make one great dish—spaghetti that was close to Rocco's.

My son Adam begs me weekly for Spaghetti Eddie. It is one of the few dishes I can make besides barbecued fish and toasted bagels. He jumps into the car with me to go to a shiny upscale super market to help pick out the ingredients. We head for the fish counter where we buy Alaskan King Crab legs, over a foot long with luscious thick meat encased in a spiny exoskeleton. Adam says, "Get two, Dad, so you and Mom can have some." We choose the rest of the seafood: Manila clams, local mussels, frozen shrimp and a small piece of halibut. Adam pleads for a California or Crunchy Roll for his typical snack. Then on to the meat counter for sausages, either chicken with basil or spicy turkey. We pick up a package of fresh linguine from the freezer and a large jar of Paul Newman pasta sauce, or several cans of diced tomatoes. Adam grabs a bag of Skittles, his favorite candy at check out. I remind him, "Don't open the bag till you finish your sushi and save at least half for after dinner," but nothing can ruin his appetite for this meal.

I wash the seafood, crack the crab, pan-fry the sausages, and throw everything into the sauce. I pick fresh oregano and basil from our spice garden along with bit of our ubiquitous rosemary and blend them into the sauce. I stir often, adding extra virgin olive oil over a low flame for at least an hour.

Growing up in a female household and a prior long-term marriage to a gourmet chef are reasons I offer for my sparse cooking repertoire, but spaghetti is my multigenerational heritage.

Adam eats all of his shellfish before he touches his pasta, shoveling huge quantities into his mouth at once.

For years I had hoped to come home from work to find a large bowl of steaming Linguini Adamo, but all too soon he became an adolescent who rarely makes his own mac n' cheese.

17

SEX IN THE GALAPAGOS

Ecuador, Spring 2006

I ARRIVED ON FERNANDINA ISLAND in the Galapagos at high tide. Suddenly the lava below me moved in several places at once. I was surrounded by hundreds of slowly crawling, camouflaged marine iguanas. They slithered through thick bird guano emanating the powerful acrid odor of digested seaweed. Aggressive male iguanas fiercely butted the heads of other males to chase them away. A female arched its tail and ran, but a large male bit her and pinned her down. Their cloacas met and one of his two penises entered her.

This day was the first on a sailing tour of the Galapagos with six other families. Our guide, Klaus, magically transformed his body into a giant tortoise, sea lion, or albatross to demonstrate animal behaviors. He had a row of dark round moles on each side of his face lined up like Orion's belt, which he pointed out our first starry equatorial night. Rare animals courting and copulating would be seen everywhere and Karen and I questioned how twelve-year-old Adam would react.

Klaus informed us this was mating season for giant tortoises. "Copulation can take several hours with loud snores and grunts from the male. These grunts are the loudest sounds in the Galapagos bush. It takes only one mating and female tortoises can store viable sperm up to ten years." Lonesome George, the most famous tortoise in the world, lives here in Puerto Ayora, Klaus explained. "He is the last one born and raised on the Island of Pinta, but no mate has been found despite a reward of $10,000." George is left only with his reputation as the world's loneliest turtle, and the revenue from the sale of his popular T-shirts.

As I climbed to the top of the bluff I saw many bright red dots in a sparsely leaved tree. Approaching the tree, I recognized the red splotches as the inflatable neck pouches of male magnificent frigate birds. Their courtship consists of aerial acrobatics, stealing nesting materials from boobies in mid-air, an ululating trill, and pumping up their shocking red pouches to at least one-fourth their body size.

Rare animals exhibiting courting and breeding behaviors were everywhere, almost to a point of embarrassment. At the top of Prince Edward's steps on Tower Island I was treated to hundreds of frigates and two types of boobies. The Nasca booby lays two eggs, but the firstborn inevitably devours the younger chick. Boobies regulate the temperature of their eggs with their webbed feet, but I feared they were crushing their eggs. Boobies often nest in bushes under the droppings of frigates' nests. I asked Klaus why and he replied, "It's just a shitty neighborhood."

On Espanola Island a male blue-footed booby performed his famous mating dance right next to me. He lifted one foot at a time and slapped it down like a clown with elongated floppy shoes. The booby bent and simultaneously pointed beak and tail to the sky, half opened its wings into a W, honked, and picked up a stick to show his skill as a nest builder. Finally, the pair clacked bills.

Flightless cormorants courted nearby, twisting their necks around each other like snakes on a stick and swaying back and forth. Albatrosses bill-fenced more tenderly than boobies. They preened each other, slid their bills together, jumped apart and met again with a clattering noise. The dance excited the birds until they secreted slippery oils, permitting their beaks to slide smoothly when they rub on top of one another.

I had expected wonders of evolution in the land mammals, but was surprised by the spectacular underwater life. We swam next to sea lion bulls, calm because it was not their mating season. Adam had never free-dove before, but he plunged deeper each day, pointing out Moorish idols to the nubile fourteen-year-old bikini clad girl in our group. I stayed close to Klaus as he surfaced and named the unusual fish we'd just seen like reef sharks and wrasse ass bass. If I couldn't find him, I'd look for the two attractive single sisters traveling with us and he'd be right next to them.

When Adam described the breeding habits of the animals of the Galapagos to his class back home, he did so without a hint of sexual tension, only snickering about the marine iguana with two penises.

18

SURVIVAL IN THE GALAPAGOS

Ecuador, Spring 2006

A SEA LION BUMPED ITS NOSE against my snorkel mask, spiraled down to the ocean floor, and then shot straight up into the air above me. Adam, just twelve, strapped his first waterproof disposable camera to his wrist and free dove ten feet to photograph the reef fish and twirl with the sea lions. An hour before the dive my wife Karen had begged Adam and me to let her stay behind in San Cristobal, fearing seasickness from the rocky boat. Now she was whooping with joy each time the sea lions barrel-rolled below despite one almost nipping her.

Klaus, our naturalist guide, told us that the sea lions may nibble because that was how they played with one another, and when they played with us they assumed our skin was as tough and resilient as theirs. These creatures even mimicked our snorkeling by blowing bubbles at us and challenging us to follow them through a loop-the-loop.

Klaus's pronouncements about the history and nature of the Galapagos lived up to his advanced billing as the naturalist for the movie *Master and Commander*. Born of a German father and Ecuadorian mother and educated in the United States, his English was tinged with touches of German and Spanish and he had a broad familiarity with American idioms.

In his first orientation talk Klaus announced "This will be the shortest week in your life" and it was. Each day had a rhythm of sameness while bringing new knowledge and wonders as we sailed the Islands on our teak-decked, three-masted schooner. A typical day started with an early morning hike when animals are most likely to be seen, and when the day is cool and the larger, more populated boats have not yet arrived. Next came an early snorkel followed by lunch, an afternoon snorkel and/or kayak, and a sunset hike followed by dinner. It is said that there is no best time to visit, but we had come under perfect conditions at the end of April: emerging from the warm, wet season, before the cool fog and two weeks after the arrival of the waved albatross.

After our underwater dance with the sea lions, we quickly changed and went back out on the rubber-inflated boat called a panga for our first hike. The frigates we observed were Klaus's favorite bird because their large wingspan-to-weight ratio (the greatest of all birds) enables them to fly sharp cutting patterns. He praised the maternal sacrifice of the female frigate, so depleted by her pregnancy and feeding her newborn that she almost dies of starvation.

Klaus lectured on the rules of the Galapagos National Park: "Don't take anything, even a grain of sand from one island to another, as even a single seed stuck on the outside of your shoe can introduce a hostile species of vegetation that will endanger the flora of the area to which it is brought. Don't use flash photography! Don't approach the animals or touch them but let them touch and approach you." The latter rule helped bring my family closer to animals than anywhere else on earth.

The red-pouched male magnificent frigate was one of the first birds I saw. It obtains nesting material wherever it can, often stealing it mid-air from the bills of boobies. It drops the twigs carelessly on the nest so that the female can rearrange them. Despite the thousands of birds here, the rain prevents guano from accumulating so I could take in the fresh, salty ocean air.

Little vegetation grew on the barren lava, but Adam's favorite was the elongated lava cactus he called "the penis plant." The individual spiny cylinders making up this hearty cactus have tips that are bright yellow and swollen.

The Galapagos marine iguana is endemic to these islands and the world's only sea-going lizard. This animal is one of many striking examples of unique species that have evolved because of the special environment of the Galapagos. It is a cold-blooded lizard that feeds in the cool waters of the Humboldt current, warming up before and after feeding by basking in the sun. This iguana feeds on algae, but also on its own feces as well as that of crabs and sea lions, adding up to quite a salty diet. They snort the extra salt out through their nostrils, the only sound they make.

Iguanas were laying eggs, as it was the end of the warm season. Their young are vulnerable to natural predators like frigate birds, herons, hawks, and snakes on land, moray eels when they feed in water, and feral dogs and cats introduced by man. A strong El Niño greatly diminishes their food supply and can devastate their population.

The only bright color that stood out against the gray lava was the bright red bill of the tropic bird, a striking small bird with white tail feathers about two feet long.

Klaus spotted a red-footed booby chick and shared that its survival required destruction of its own sibling. This prompted him to talk about aggression and survival in the Galapagos. "A male booby that cannot find a mate may attack and rape a female booby, but we should not be quick to anthropomorphize," he said, explaining that now that we have pretty much eliminated man as the main predator, we have only to deal with predation by the animals he left behind. There are very few natural extra-species predators in the Galapagos except for the hawk and owl.

A Galapagos hawk, the main natural predator of the islands, perched nearby on a tree stump. It was the larger female, which typically mates with four males that all help with incubation and rearing of the chicks. There are only about 800 of these birds in existence, but I saw quite a few and the cockiness of their perching style meant they knew they were the bosses of these islands.

The flightless cormorant, another species that evolved and is endemic to the Galapagos, also nested in Fernandina. Adam and I had grown used to the cormorants back home diving to steal the fish we had caught, but this species had stubby, almost vestigial wings, allowing it to plunge deeper than its northern cousins.

We hiked on Isabella Island to hunt for the Galapagos Giant Tortoise but only saw one about eight inches across, which reminded me of long-forgotten Myrtle, the turtle I found and kept for a summer when I was younger than Adam is now. We saw our first land iguanas here, easily distinguished from the marine variety by their yellow skin and wizened faces, looking even more prehistoric than their marine cousins. Males of this species copulate violently, seizing the female by the neck in order to mate.

Darwin finches were everywhere on Isabella. There are thirteen species of finches in the Galapagos, each with a beak adapted to the availability of food in the area they inhabit, be it small, medium and large seeds, nectar, fruit, or insects. It is these finches—nondescript black, gray and brown birds—that taught Darwin about adaptive radiation and established a foundation for the theory of the evolution of man.

Because of the isolation of the islands, the native animals here are almost all reptiles; in the rest of the world, most are mammals. Only reptiles, which can go a long time without water, could make the 600-mile journey from the mainland. The only native land mammal here is the rice rat, which is in danger of being wiped out by its man-introduced cousin, the black or ship rat.

Whalers looking for a meat source ate Galapagos Giant Tortoises and later introduced goats as a food source to Isabella and several other islands in the nineteenth century. Thousands of feral goats roamed many islands, destroying the foliage and leaving a barren desert that could not support animal life until a goat eradication program began in 1965. Since then, goats have been eliminated from several islands but are still rampant on others.

Feral cats have succeeded goats on several islands and are much more difficult to extinguish. Wild dogs prey on young tortoises, tortoise eggs, land and marine iguanas, and penguins. In 1970 a pack of wild dogs attacked a large colony of land iguanas and destroyed over 500. Some aspects of the destruction of native species are subtler, like the distribution of guava seeds by cattle, so that guava overwhelms native flora.

On the fifth day of our sail we took the panga to Santiago Island. Most of our boatmen were already on shore and I noticed they were joined by crews from several other boats just above us on a bluff to our left. I could just make out the corner of a soccer goal post on the edge of a plateau. After several days at sea, the crews were all meeting for their weekly soccer game. I watched them jump off the boats onto shore, dribbling their soccer balls in deft moves behind their backs and using their knees to keep the ball in the air. There were shouts of joy from the players when we arrived for our hike.

Pigs were brought to this island by farmers. They eventually became wild and ate so many tortoise eggs that tortoises became extinct here. Fur Seals had become almost extinct on Santiago because nineteenth century whalers killed hundreds of thousands for their fur. Their population has rebounded, despite a setback from a recent El Niño. The fur seals have adapted to their environment for survival. They feed on fish and squid at night to avoid competing with the sea lions and iguanas and, to avoid the sharks, eat much less when the moon is full.

Santa Cruz Island has a population of 11,000 and includes much of the three percent of the land of the Galapagos that is not in the national park. This island is a good teacher of what can happen to the flora and fauna of an area when a non-native species is introduced. Many animals introduced by man onto this island have become wild. Feral dogs, pigs, cats, donkeys, and goats have destroyed native foliage and turtle eggs. Elephant grass, lantana and guava trees spread rampant over the fields. These alien species were introduced rapidly before the native fauna and flora had a chance to adapt to them.

On Santa Cruz we walked along a bucolic bay where hundreds of boobies and swallowtail gulls were gathered along the shore. Sea lions surfed in the sea just below us. "Surfing is part of their play," Klaus told us. "Animals at the top of the food chain are more likely to play, but only ten percent of male sea lions have offspring. So you can only mate as a sea lion if you expend enough energy to be an alpha male." As he said this, a spectacular blowhole erupted right in front of the surfing sea lions.

Klaus led the group in a left turn, heading inland where just around a bend I saw my first albatross, and just beyond it a nesting colony of hundreds of these wrongly maligned birds. Albatross are monogamous though they may not see each other for years spent at sea between meetings on the island of Espanola, where they return to mate. The waved albatross is the largest bird that breeds in the Galapagos and there are about 12,000 pairs that breed here. They bill-fenced right in front of our group, much more tenderly than the boobies were in their courtship.

I had anticipated the wonder of the land animals of the Galapagos, but the underwater spectacle was a total surprise from the first moment we danced with the sea lions. The rich undersea life of the Islands is a function of their equatorial location at the confluence of three major currents: The Humboldt, which brings cool water that is rich in nutrients from the sub-arctic, the cool Cromwell with its equatorial undercurrent, and the warm waters of El Niño. The deep, cool Humboldt upwells when it hits the Galapagos, producing a surprisingly cool air temperature at the equator. El Niño occurs every year, generally bringing rain to the Galapagos between January and March. Some years there is a drought, which benefits the marine animals, and other times as in 1997-1998 and 1982-1983 the rain is so heavy that large numbers of sea animals like marine iguanas and sea lions die, as do boobies, which depend on the sea for food. In these years, land species like birds, butterflies, and land iguanas flourish. These two recent El Niños, apparently influenced by global warming, were unprecedented in their intensity and destructiveness.

In my first dives I recognized old friends like moorish idols, angelfish and surgeonfish. Klaus showed a slide show of species new to me, like damselfish, blue chin parrotfish, Mexican monkfish, and rainbow wrasse, helping me recognize them on my dives. My underwater viewing was greatly enhanced by proximity to larger animals like fur seals and sea turtles. Often there would be a large turtle in the water floating elegantly just beneath me, and cormorants, penguins and sea lions right above.

Although I'd snorkeled with Karen many times before this, she was now vastly more comfortable and had no need to hold my hand for reassurance. She also had a throwaway disposable camera, and in contrast to the great discretion she shows when photographing on land, she used all twenty-seven shots the first day. Proclaiming her love for snorkeling, her enthusiasm grew with each dive. Karen's prior competitive swimming helped her to eventually dive more deeply than anyone on the boat except Klaus.

Klaus was at his best underwater, particularly when he strapped on his weight belt and dove at least 15 feet, pointing out fish, sea stars and iridescent sea urchins. He broke off a claw from a crab and dangled it to entice an octopus out of a cave, which shot its tentacles out for a split second, all it took to grab the crab. I was able to catch a peek at its bright orange-yellow-brown body and white-cupped tentacles.

Starfish were startlingly colorful, particularly the chocolate chip and red cushion variety. Higher in the water column I saw a school of small barracuda sharks, but these were not at all frightening compared to the five-foot Whitetip reef shark I saw wriggling beneath me the next day.

Klaus pumped up expectations about our last day's free dive, telling us "Last week at this spot, there were huge bonita, sting rays, and a school of hammerhead sharks," but

I didn't see a hammerhead on that dive, only a sea turtle and a school of damselfish. We made up for it in our afternoon snorkel, particularly Adam, who spotted a stone scorpion fish and a six-foot trumpet fish.

After I recalled all the animals I had seen and been so close to, and when I thought about their struggle to survive, I realized that if we are not capable of preserving our heritage on the Galapagos, we might be well on the way to turning our planet over to feral goats and black rats.

19

Catalina Island:
An Adventure Close To Home
Catalina Island, 2006

An immense hairy bison blocked me from leading a group of twelve sixth graders on the path intended for a nature hike. I turned to Leah, our California Marine Institute guide, and pleaded for help. She threw a few stones toward the beast to persuade it to move off our path, taking care not to toss one close enough to startle it. She succeeded only in provoking the buffalo to amble closer so we backed away and took a different path.

The prehistoric creature lingered throughout our stay, resting in the middle of the grounds while dozens of excited sixth graders cautiously snapped photos from a respectful distance.

Adam's science teacher chose Catalina for Thurston Middle School's field trip, she said, "so students could experience what Laguna Beach ecology was like 200 years ago." Thurston's first session on the island took place November 2003, a memorable trip because ninety students suffered severe gastrointestinal symptoms from a strain of the Norwalk flu. The trip earned the name the Catalina Hurl and commemorative Hurl T-shirts enjoyed brief popularity in Laguna Beach.

There are several myths about the arrival of buffalo on Catalina, such as they were brought to kill the snakes or to make buffalo burgers, but the real story is that they were transported to Catalina to make a movie eighty-two years ago. After the movie was finished, it was too expensive to remove them from the island so they have remained a fascinating though non-native attraction of Catalina ever since. Only fourteen bison were brought over to make one scene for a film that was cut and never shown. The herd grew to an eco-threatening 500 head at one point, since they eat both native and non-native plants and their coats trap and spread non-native seeds throughout the island. The ideal buffalo population for the island is 150 so several hundred were shipped to South Dakota at great expense.

Leah told the group that if they didn't complain about the hike, they could have a special swim at the end. The hike was hot for all and boring for most of them but the kids didn't complain. Leah taught about endemic species on the island like the Catalina Island Fox. There were 1,300 foxes on the island until a canine distemper virus killed 1,200. A vaccination and recovery program brought their numbers back to above 300.

The promised treat was diving off the dock into 65-degree water, holding hands and shouting our new group name "Foxy Bison Bunch." At first I loved jumping into the water as much as the kids, but they kept diving and screaming our group name long after I had quit.

The sixth graders were initiated into ocean biology through a long introductory lecture made bearable by costumes and games in which kids were splashed by water from a barrel, and the speakers had buckets of water poured on them by colleagues on the roof above. The kids pointed, warned and yelled like at a Punch and Judy Show.

By our second day, the water temperature had risen another three degrees to an almost balmy sixty-eight. Nevertheless, we all donned thick three-piece wet suits with booties and hoods then spent a smothering hour in our extra-thick suits listening to the last part of the orientation. Leah led us in exercising and stretching before we hit the water. One of the girls in the group, Natalie, had never been in the ocean despite living two blocks away from it. I knew this could be trouble. Leah was very patient, slowly introducing Natalie to snorkeling. Once Leah left her side, Natalie panicked and gasped for air. Leah motioned to me to take her back to shore on the rescue boogie board I was towing. This snorkel was the first time any of these kids had ever experienced diving in a kelp forest. Adam loved it, and with Leah's help we saw opal eyes and glorious gold garibaldi, the California state fish. We could see as well in this crystal clear water as in the waters of the Galapagos.

After a lunch of corn dogs, french fries, and Kool-Aid, a meal rescued for me by a salad bar, we headed back into the water for kayaking. I was teamed with Natalie, who had never kayaked before. She and I, like the rest of the group, adorned ourselves with blue and green war paint. We colored our faces and bodies with aggressive whoops and hollers, knowing the paint was intended to prepare for war with other groups of kayakers. Natalie sat up front and followed my instructions perfectly so we could maneuver slowly. We stayed out of the battle because Natalie certainly would have panicked if our kayak had sunk. The boys on each team attacked the girls on the other side as if they were pirates sinking ships to capture bounty and slaves. Just as the boys began to board, the girls shrieked at the top of their lungs, cries of great delight as well as quaking fear.

A voluntary night snorkel, billed as the high point of the week, topped off this very full day. We used luminescent tubes attached to our snorkels so we could be observed from shore by the lifeguard and carried high-powered underwater flashlights. Our leader strapped on a weight belt so she could free dive despite her thick and highly buoyant wet suit. The kelp forests were as pitch black as anywhere I had ever been until we switched on our searchlights. When we spotted something of interest, we moved our beams

Catalina Island

in a circle to share the viewing with other divers. Adam motioned me over to see a huge prehistoric-looking crusty crab, which Leah brought up for us, bravely holding it by its back. We spotted stingrays, leopard sharks, halibut, and a huge calico bass. The garibaldi were even more spectacular at night and several of the kids shouted "Look at the Ghirardellis!"

Snorkeling continued the next day, this time with weight belts, a first for Adam as well as for me. A change in the current left the water murky so our visibility was much closer to zero than the sixty feet Catalina is famous for. I hesitated to dive fearing I'd get entangled in the thick kelp, but I found some openings I could safely explore. We learned that the kelp was not just a morass of green but was made up of root-like structures called "holdfasts" and a system of air bladders. We were warned not to pop them because doing so damages the kelp's ability to make food and grow its normal two feet a day. The kelp, which can grow to 100 feet tall, hides and feeds several species of bass, snail, and perch.

Adam always ended up walking with and sitting next to Lilly, who is the kind of girl every son's mother and father wants their boy to end up with: smart, pretty, kind, creative, and graceful, with long, blonde hair that falls to the middle of her back. She chided Adam to act normally saying, "If you act weird, I'll pinch you."

The following day when Adam was awkward, mute

and immobile in a vain attempt to not act strangely, Lilly said, "I changed my mind. I'm not going to pinch you. That would be too weird." Adam denied that he felt any differently about her than he did any of his other friends, male or female. Only nine months earlier, when the fall semester began, Adam had shared a discovery: "Mom, the girls have a line down the middle of their chest now!"

Environmental preservation was taught by having the students problem-solve in groups. They learned that after almost becoming extinct from DDT in the Pacific, twenty bald eagles have survived on the island; they learned that wild goats and pigs are destructive to the flora of the island and have had to be eradicated, just like those in the Galapagos.

We studied plankton under a microscope where the kids saw tiny jellyfish and sea cucumbers and learned that plankton makes 70 percent of the oxygen we breathe. The students made a collage of different colors of algae. When they were asked to depict their favorite activity on Catalina, Natalie depicted us kayaking, her main area of mastery on the island.

Several of the other chaperones told me about a "night show" that was not to be missed. I took Adam and his friends Nick and Ryan to the end of the pier at 8:45. Adam shouted, "Look! There's a flying fish!" Suddenly there were schools of them skipping across the water. Many were being chased by sea lions but others were just flying,

flying higher and longer than any I had ever seen before.

In contrast to my first trip alone with Adam to Alaska, one that had been so traumatic for him, this was Adam in his element—his friends, his marine environment, his water sports, and even his friendly school principal. Of course he flourished and I was there to see it all, to get to know his old friends better and to meet his new ones. He and I shared several unique experiences: snorkeling at night, diving with weight belts, and discovering we didn't have to travel to the Galapagos to see unique species evolving on an island. We saw even more clearly here that the marine ecosystem surrounding Catalina and other islands must survive or the extensive production of oxygen provided by plankton will be slowly eliminated. To learn this we only had to travel eighteen miles from home to an island we see on the horizon almost every day.

20

Himba Happiness

Namibia, Summer 2006

WE HOP DOWN FROM THE BACK of an aging powder-blue truck and step into a three-hut Himba village in northern Namibia. Only the narrow Kunene River separates us from Angola.

The huts are small, packed with family members and made of sticks, mud, and odorless dried cow dung. Our guide, Koos, proposes that Karen cover her skin with a local ointment of ochre, milk fat, and herbs that smell like rotten butter. As soon as she coats all the exposed parts of her body, the villagers roar approval at her brown-stained flesh and gesture to her to paint and bare her breasts as they have done for centuries. Karen's few unpainted parts show a modest blush. She feels giddy, abandoning her inhibitions while maintaining her limits. The villagers bob their heads and giggle at her embarrassment.

All the women are bare-chested at the next village we visit except for one who pulls her long, faded print skirt up over her chest when we dismount from the truck. She is a healer who has crossed a crocodile-infested river to tend to an ailing villager. She cracks a whip to startle a herd of cows into line before heading for a hut where the tribe is clapping, chanting and singing. She is more aloof than anyone I have met in this embracing country, freezing me with a look that says, "Don't mess with me!" Women sitting outside the hut keep rhythm with the music as they shake gourds to separate fat from milk.

Our next stop is a school attended by local students dressed in stiff blue and white uniforms. They have left behind their milk-soaked animal-hide garments, ochre-stained skin and bangles to attend classes for the time being, if not for the rest of their lives. Karen and I enter a classroom while Adam goes off with Koos. When we emerge, we observe students bouncing and screeching. Koos has set up a track in the deep sand, and Adam is getting ready to race against five boys and a girl, all older, taller, used to walking miles to school and running barefoot in sand. Adam whispers to me, "They are so fast. They train by running from crocodiles."

The Himba teenagers shake their hands and feet in excitement. Adam rocks back and forth, stretching his calves. Koos bellows "Go!" and the runners take off. Adam gets a late start but picks up steam and passes two boys just before collapsing into the sand after crossing the finish line. The winner stands tall and proud. He stuns me when he says, "If Adam had beaten me, I would not have eaten again for my entire life."

The aroma of ochre and milk fat lingered on Karen's skin during the day-long flight home and remained for months on the bracelets and woodcarvings we brought back to our home and offices. Tempered with time, the milky scent of the rich Himba culture wafts back to me from the wooden headrest on my desk.

21

Papua Pride

Papua New Guinea, August 2007

Hundreds of Waghi villagers rushed to meet Karen, Adam, and me as our Jeep pulled up to the base of a mountain in the highlands of Papua New Guinea.

We scaled the mountain surrounded by an army of smiling helpers who offered their outstretched palms to guide us up the muddy slope. When we reached the summit, the Waghi placed garlands of red and yellow bush flowers around our necks and formed two lines to define our path. We danced through their queues into the village to the rhythmic sound of a Jew's harp played by a village elder, his eyes circled by rich black and white paint above the wide black stripes across his cheekbones. Animal pelts covered the shoulders of the village chief, surrounding his necklace of boar's tusks. Children, dressed in raggedy T-shirts and shorts, clapped and waved with beaming smiles. Topless elderly women embraced us with tears streaming down their cheeks. The contagion of their emotion choked me up, but I held back not quite knowing what to make of their surprisingly intense feelings. I learned we were the first tourists to visit in eight months. Did relief prompt their emotions, or was it genuine joy at having visitors from far away?

Wispy pine trees surrounded our lodge and continued down a slope to a river flowing 6,500 feet above sea level. A few fragile wooden posts supported the second story of the building; its walls were made of thinly woven bamboo and the floors, a touch thicker, indented wherever I walked. I opened the door to our room (gently, I thought, but I can be quite clumsy) and the wood ripped off its hinges. Three workmen came to fix the damage, bopping to the African music Karen played on her iPod while they worked. We washed our hands in a communal basin, sanitation concerns masked by the fruity odor of grape soap for the women and sweet rose petal for the men. The walls were so thin I could hear every sound in the guesthouse. Karen kept waking me up to jar me from snoring, though I mumbled it was surely someone else in our group. I had the runs our first night, as did several guests, so the noise and trembling of footfalls kept most of us awake.

In the morning, Adam greeted the others with,

"Good morning, did you have diarrhea last night?" One member of our group left before breakfast, concerned about sanitation and fearful of falling through the floor. He had asked the tour company to rescue us but no one else wanted to leave.

The Australian government gave PNG it's independence in 1975 but continues to exert influence. The Aussies recently initiated large multi-tribal competitive singsings as a substitute for clan wars. The villagers staged a special singsing for us. These celebrations preserve their heritage by providing an opportunity to wear traditional dress and body paint, which are still used to intimidate the enemy before battle. Only a few decades ago these were preparation for headhunting raids.

Waghi display their wealth by wearing their best feathers and shells, often borrowed from extended family. The assistant tribal leader wore necklaces made of Kina shells and a headdress with massive eagle feathers as if coming out of both sides of his head. The dancers wore brightly colored striped headbands and their armbands bristled with leaves and flowers. Longer leaves hung down from their waistbands (informally called CYA, or cover-your-ass grass). Many had red and yellow horizontal stripes on their cheekbones and vertical stripes on their chins, and most wore big black cassowary feathers in their headbands.

The marchers entered our area by stepping backwards, then sashaying back and forth and hopping to the rhythm of a drumbeat of alternating slaps and thrusts. Their bare feet were huge and almost as broad as long. I experienced them as powerful and intimidating though few of them were taller than Adam's five-foot-one.

Dozens of people gathered around Karen and Adam as they bargained to purchase fifty cents worth of candy. Adam felt uncomfortable at being stared at so he decided to become more active. First he balanced his walking stick in the palm of his hand. A large group of kids thronged over to watch him steady his pole in the air. His sun-bleached blond hair shone in the cloud-filtered sun and his deep dimples flashed; he took charge. Soon there were several hundred locals of all ages watching him and laughing at everything he did, and he was milking it.

Adam stabilized his stick on two fingers then on one. He did quite well, but each time it toppled they all roared with laughter. He blindfolded himself with his surf team sweatshirt and still balanced the pole. He zipped off the legs of his cargo pants as the onlookers pointed at his knees with waggling index fingers. He placed the pant legs on his arms, pulled the sleeves of his jacket up over his legs and still balanced the stick. By the end of his performance he had an audience of 300 highlanders howling.

We returned to the lodge, where Adam quickly became bored of reading and was relieved to hear distant chants of "Adam, Adam." He ran to the children who were calling his name and played rolling-down-the-hill games with the locals. When they settled down he was taught pidgin, the one common tongue of Papua New Guinea's 850-plus languages. I was proud of Adam's amazing resilience in what could easily have been an uncomfortable situation for a thirteen-year-old.

We brought out our iPod and speakers and danced with the locals. The chief joined in and everyone clapped and screamed. Karen discovered a young boy who could do a few Motown steps and danced with him and two sisters who had stayed by her side and sung to her all day. I did the Twist and the Waghi cheered like it was the greatest dance they'd ever seen. Karen taught them the Bump, which they blended into their own movements. Eventually, when the iPod battery ran out, local drummers, singers, and dancers took over the pace, hopping and circling and linking arms with us. Even though I had no costume on, I felt part of the singsing.

Karen gave reversible, brightly printed skirts to the sisters, Anita and Elise. They returned in a half hour and gave her necklaces made from beads, shells, and the toothy jawbone of a small animal. Adam and I each received a smaller chain of shells.

We had seen courtship dances in many of the other villages we'd visited in PNG and those had felt quite staged. The Waghi now invited us to their own romantic dance as a farewell performance for our group. We entered a darkened low-ceilinged hut with a fire pit in the center of a circle.

Facing the ring were nine women, two with uncovered breasts, all wearing short grass skirts. Karen, Adam, and I squeezed onto log seats in the rear of the tiny hut while the women sang "I need to fill the space in my heart and next to me." The girls chanted, clapped, laughed, and trilled until their pleas were answered. Eight muscular bare-chested young men dressed in grass skirts quickly filled the spaces next to the women, though they faced away from the fire so that when they leaned back their eyes met the eyes of the women. The men wriggled, shimmied, and shook pre-orgastically; the females slapped and rubbed the men who put their thighs over those of the women next to them as they nestled and stroked each other. I hadn't seen any of these dancers around the village so this may have been an imported courting ceremony. Even so, we hustled Adam out of there before an orgy erupted.

After three nights we assembled for a formal farewell at a dirt field in the village center. The chief, now in shabby clothes though still wearing his potent necklace, said with emotion cracking his voice, "I have truly gotten to know you in just a few days. I feel so sad that you are leaving." When he finished, he began to cry. Next to his feet was a baby pig held by a rope leash. The chief said they'd all agreed that the pig should go to Adam because he had become one of them.

"The pig will be named Adam. We will take care of it and feed it everyday. When Adam returns in five years, he will kill the pig himself and we will have a great feast." He then proceeded to give each of the other tourists a gift of a necklace. I removed my favorite cap and T-shirt and gave them to the chief. The villagers formed a line and we shook each of their hands and said goodbye. Anita, Elise, and their mother, whom we hadn't met, sobbed uncontrollably. Most of them were in tears and this time so was I. On our way down the hill, Adam shared that the gift of a pig was a greater honor than his surfing trophies. He too had tears in his eyes, but he ran ahead to hide his emotions from us.

22

To Live and Die in Varanasi

India, Christmas 2008

A THIN AND BEDRAGGLED OARSMAN rows his decaying wooden boat north to a crematory. No burning bodies here. We pass early morning bathers courting good fortune by bathing in the soapy, toothpaste-bubbled, ash-laden Ganges in the freezing, foggy morning air.

The oarsman steers Adam, Karen, and me past a holy man whose followers include a dozen small children singing songs like the young boys in *Slumdog Millionaire* just before they were rendered blind to enhance their begging. The rower skillfully turns the boat in the opposite direction.

Temple bells and conch shell horns celebrate the dawning of a new day. Worn stone palaces, each with their own broad concrete staircase down to the water's edge, line the river. Signs advertising that they are now B&B's front many of the structures.

We reach the endpoint of our ride, a bustling crematorium with smoke rising from three separate pyres. Two corpses, one wrapped in white and the other in faded orange linen, lie waiting their turn. I am certain I saw the white shrouded body the night before mounted on bamboo poles and carried past me through the streets in a funeral procession. Sizzling smoke from the smoldering corpses mingles with the smells of burning camphor, incense, and the sweat of the boatman.

Bodies burn on the slabs for hours, after which the lower caste workers sift through the remains for remnants of gold teeth and rings. Ashes are placed in two piles by the riverbank; one black and smoking, the other gray and still, to be shortly washed into the river. Adam leans as close as he can to the pyre. "I can see the head and hair, Dad," he proclaims gleefully.

I am surprised that I do not experience the unmistakable odor of burning hair. An attendant beckons us closer, but I lead Adam away and past the holy men along the street above us. Karen snaps amazing photographs of the more subtly adorned pilgrims.

Just a few days before this I had observed a Bengal tiger on the prowl. Seeing this animal in the wild was one of the experiences that I had wanted to achieve before I die. I had accomplished this, but the sighting lost its life-affirming quality in the face of so much death along the banks of the Ganges.

Karen confronted me, Buddhist follower that she is. "You need to meditate to follow the rise and fall of all of life, like your breath," she said. "In this way you cultivate the internal condition necessary to accept impermanence. Your soul is what is important. I hope Varanasi has taught you how unimportant your body is."

I wanted so much to believe this. I could acknowledge that I would eventually be only ash, dust, and memories, that my life had been full and I could let go, but emptiness tugged at me, raw and gnawing.

23

MERCY MURSI

Southern Ethiopia, Summer 2008

KAREN, ADAM, NOW FOURTEEN, and I huddled in the back seat of an aging Toyota Land Cruiser and listened to our guide Dereje's tales of the Mursi people as we entered their tribal territory. We stopped at a flimsy barrier to open the cargo gate so that a slender park guard toting an antiquated single-shot rifle could find a seat for himself on a set of blue tarps in the back of the SUV.

Dereje resumed his briefing: "The Mursi are without mercy. They are fierce enemies of all the surrounding tribes. They strut around their villages with Kalashnikov AK-47s strapped on their shoulders, rifles that are capable of shooting 600 rounds a minute. They used to duel to the death with six-foot long poles, but now the Mursi fight until they are totally exhausted or in pain from broken fingers." He explained that the men cover their bodies with chalk markings and demand payment for every click of your camera.

We arrived at a group of Mursi huts and drove in even though several cars full of tourists were already there, snapping pictures and racing from one tribal member to another. Locals thronged around us demanding "two bir," about 20 cents, for a photo, "water" as barter, and "five" as the price of an embossed and often chipped women's ceramic lip plate.

Men arrogantly carrying shiny Kalashnikovs roamed the village in groups of threes and fours. A woman stood proudly with her own automatic rifle, strings of bullets woven into her hair, twenty gold bracelets on each arm.

The women were powerful and noble with impressive clay inserts placed in their erect lower lips. When they removed the plate the lower lip fell slack and limp, dangling below the chin; it was so flexible that if extended the lip could be pulled up and over the head.

One lip-plated woman who carried a frail baby had hair decorated with dangling corncobs. Karen fiddled with her camera before she snapped the picture and offered "two bir." The woman vigorously shook her head. "No," she said, "one more for baby and *ten* for the big camera." Karen burst out, "I can't take pictures here. These people are too aggressive." We secured our cameras in the car, the Italians left, the village became calm, and we were free to roam.

Mercy Mursi

The women of the village were uniformly topless and took a keen interest in seeing Karen's bra and breasts. Adam ran over to me. "Mom's showing them her breasts!" I raced over to where several women milled around my wife to find them taking turns looking down her blouse. "Did you show them your breasts?" I asked in disbelief. She beamed back. "Sure, they showed theirs, so I showed mine. We're like birds showing off our feathers."

With no shyness in this village, adolescent girls surrounded Adam and me. They had ear discs in their lower lobes but none in their lips because they were not yet 15, the usual age to begin lip stretching.

At first the girls playfully tied a rubber band around Adam's neck and pretended to tighten it. Then they pointed at his chest, his surfer's pectoral muscles protruding from his thin body, and teased him about whether he was a boy or a girl. The young girls' breasts were all firm and high. Those of the older women were flat and sagging. Perhaps this is why all the women found Karen's, which were neither, so interesting.

There was less frenzy about selling us their crafts than taking pictures, and after Karen purchased a set of lip plates and she and Adam bought copper bangles, we were free to mingle and interact. Karen kissed Adam on the cheek. "The Mursi don't understand this way of showing affection," Dereje said. "Their way is to gently pull on each other and laugh."

I noticed a European man drifting between the groups and taking pictures of tourist interaction with the Mursi. I initiated a conversation and learned that Tomas was a Hungarian doctoral candidate from Leeds University in England. He had first stayed at another village to learn the language before moving in with this group a few weeks ago. They were almost finished building his hut of sticks and mud, identical to theirs.

"I had to pay everyone in the village for making my hut," he said, "but they told me it wasn't safe for me to pitch my tent outside their village as another group of Mursi might attack me."

His thesis topic was the effects of tourism on the Mursi, which also interested me so I spent most of my second hour in the village with him. Tomas already spoke the language and served as my translator. I asked if he experienced the Mursi's attitude towards tourists as aggressive.

"Not really," he replied. "They are used to tourists coming for only half an hour. Since they have such a short time, the Mursi feel pressured to demand as much money as they can as quickly as possible."

One Mursi woman sat by the shade of her hut, dressed in plain white clothing and not willing to be photographed by tourists. She asked Tomas, "Why are they still here? Why is he writing like you?"

He responded, "They want to get to know you."

The woman in white countered, "Then why don't

they stay here with us like you do?" I thought this was a very good question, one that led me to ponder the merits of creature comforts versus a more authentic experience.

Tomas said the Mursi women have a lot of power. The men turn the money over to them and the women are only beaten if they are unfaithful. Males have six or seven children with each of several wives, often one child every year. Though they stay in separate huts, the wives form close bonds with each other to help them deal with the strong males. If a husband dies, the wife is first offered to his brother. Dereje later said that if Tomas had an affair with a married Mursi woman, he'd be killed on the spot.

There are many theories about the the lip plates of the Mursi women. The most common is that the bigger the lip disc, the more cattle they are awarded for their bride price. A Mursi husband stated this was true only in the sense that women with bigger plates tend to be photographed more and in this way are worth more heads of cattle.

Another theory is that this was done to make women unattractive to slave traders. It is clear that slitting their lips still demarcates entrance into the adult world, as it has for centuries. What a contrast the women's lip plates make with the men's modern automatic rifles!

My mom would have had a really hard time with this journey.

24

TOUCHED BY A GORILLA

Rwanda, Summer 2009

Agashya, a 400-pound silverback gorilla, finishes the last of his bamboo shoots and rumbles straight for our group of seven tourists. The dense, damp, mossy forest leaves me no room to back up. Eugene, a Rwandan park ranger, commands softly but urgently "Get down!" I crouch, duck my head into my chest, and scrunch my eyes shut.

Karen snaps a photo of a grey and black mass just before she kneels. We have no idea where our fifteen-year-old son Adam is! He's so good in these situations that he'll figure it out, I keep telling myself. I feel the tips of the silverback's hairs and breathe in his strangely sweet odor as he brushes by me and moves to the edge of the clearing where Adam is filming and has no place to go. He quickly slides his thin body between the thick bamboo stalks into a protective cave of green brush. After the gorilla passes him, trackers machete away an exit door and Adam emerges with a dimpled grin.

Adam pushes against me to get a better position for his video when Agashya ignores us and joins his many mates and babies. I look closely at his face with my binoculars until his eyes meet mine. I drop the binos quickly. The younger gorillas beat their chests and come toward us. Eugene moves us back five feet and the infants retreat, only to advance again. Tourists are instructed to stay at least twenty-three feet from the animals, but the gorillas don't follow these warnings.

I realize that Marianna, a veteran of over twenty treks, is standing next to me and clearing her throat to make Dian Fossey-like sounds that say to the animals "Don't worry about me. Do not be frightened." She opens her eyes wide and lifts her eyebrows. I watch her facial expressions turn into those of the baby gorilla. Marianna whispers to them in an oddly soothing Bavarian dialect. Tears slowly stream down her cheeks when the babies come close and tilt their heads toward her. She shares with me that her husband of forty years died after their last trek together three years ago and they have no children. The infant gorillas back away from Marianna to suckle at their mother's breast, then climb weak vines and collapse to the ground where they twirl and wrestle. Marianna coos to them and they scramble our way again. She smiles happily. I quiver, envious of her connection. Adam's adolescent rebellion is rapidly distancing him from his mom and me, but our shared experience with the gorilla family has brought us together, at least for the moment.

What is so special about these animals, I wonder, that they can rescue the economy of a small nation or entice me to hike up the steepest mountain I have ever climbed? Gorillas share so much of our DNA that when they scratch their head, hiccup, or pick their teeth they remind me of my Uncle Joe. Yet they are quite dangerous if not habituated by years of loving contact with trackers. There are no bars, moats, or car doors between these huge beasts and us; it is only reciprocal trust that protects us both from each other.

25

Lalibela Liturgy

Northern Ethiopia, Summer 2009

My grandmother wore her hair in a tight gray bun, but I never forgot the one time she loosened every strand, letting it tumble to her waist. She brought me with her to a small orthodox Jewish synagogue where she sat upstairs, and at eight years old I watched in awe from below. She sang, she rocked, she was aware of nothing but her prayers; she was transformed.

The next time I experienced religious ecstasy would be more than sixty years later at the Orthodox Christian Temple of Emmanuel in Lalibela, Ethiopia. Chanting had gone on for seven hours by the time my family arrived at 10 a.m. This miraculous church was carved out of a mountain by as many as 40,000 workers, maybe with the help of several angels in a single day. I was shocked when I heard the chant. It sounded less Catholic, more Hebrew.

The three of us sat quietly just outside the circle of praying, drumming, and dancing men for an hour. The priests motioned me into their circle. I looked toward Karen, who shook her head and said, "You go in. This is a man's thing."

A monk handed me a long cruciate prayer stick and a small wooden musical instrument with two miniature cymbals that made a tinny noise. A sympathetic worshiper caught my eye and motioned to me when to sit, stand, or shake my cymbals. Just as I found my rhythm, Karen joined me while Adam stayed back and filmed. An ululating trill punctured the steady rhythm of the chanting. I rocked and shuffled to the prayer, mouthing syllables I didn't understand just like in Temple decades ago.

A procession of deacons wrapped in rich red cloth under gold brocade vestments emerged from the battered wooden church door. One carried a Bible. Another carefully shielded the holy book from the sun with an umbrella. They paraded inside the circle holding the Bible out to be kissed by all the priests. I felt I was back in synagogue edging toward the aisle to kiss the Torah with my prayer shawl.

The deacon carrying the holy book approached me, but passed by. My helper-priest saw the look of disappointment on my face and motioned the man with the Bible to turn back to me so I could kiss it. The moment I kissed that sacred book I felt the ecstasy of the oneness of all religions that the rhythm of the liturgy had been building within me throughout the ceremony. Later on I learned the priests were not praying in Latin but in an ancient Semitic tongue.

That night I dreamt I was driving my family to Cape Canaveral to take a rocket to the moon. My car turned into a motorized wheel chair and I felt lost and unable to get it to work. Could my dream be questioning if my trips to esoteric destinations would get me where I needed to go?

26

Sundays with Senya

Brooklyn Heights, New York—Fall 2009

I HAD MY FIRST GRANDCHILD when I had doubled the age my kid sister was when she had her first grandchild.

I visited Senya for his second birthday, six months after the last time, anticipating that he wouldn't remember me. His pop-pop, Rodney, lives a subway ride away and plays with him every Sunday. I feared that compared with him, I'd be the forgotten granddad. Could I get enough recognition to tap the love I knew I felt for Senya?

I tentatively rang the bell to my son Tony's modest 28th floor, East River-view apartment. Inside the door I heard a melodious, high voice say, "Papa Ed. Papa Ed." I've never been called that before, and his loving tone melted me instantly. This is why everyone wants grandkids! It helps that he is gorgeous, but aren't they all?

Senya had shoulder-length chestnut brown hair, huge blue eyes and, like all the boys in my family, dimples. He unabashedly tugged me through every room in the house, showing me all the places he had taken over with his toys and books. When we sat next to each other, he steadily pushed me back down to an inch from the seat of my chair. I pleaded with him to let me up until he firmly pulled me next to his warm, sweet body.

We did many activities together I hadn't done since my older sons Alex and Tony were toddlers. I pushed and ever so gently whirled him on the tire swing at his neighborhood park, and he loved the dizzy high kids get from being spun. I read Richard Scarry's *Cars and Trucks* aloud and praised him when he found Goldbug on every page. We went to the Central Park Zoo, where we laughed at the monkeys and I saw my first snow lion. Back home we moved Thomas The Tank Engine back and forth on a wooden track and smashed toy cars on the floor. With each game we played, I fought back tears of longing for the identical games I'd played with my older boys so long ago.

I took him to the toy store and said, "Pick out any toy you want," and was not surprised when he chose the same set of five fire trucks that each of my three sons would have selected. He grabbed a scooter and charged through the store, scattering adults wherever he rode. Before we made our final decision, we went on the Internet in their apartment and read reviews of every toddler vehicle on the market. At last, a parenting experience that wasn't déjà vu.

The following Sunday, I Skyped Senya and he greeted me with an endearing "Papa Ed." I watched him ride his stabilized three-wheel scooter around the apartment, dwarfed by a huge helmet adorned with pictures of cars. His face lit up. I hoped he could feel my smile.

Now he knows who Papa Ed is.

27

My Thai Grandson

Phuket, Thailand—Spring 2010

If a seer had told me at my Bar Mitzvah that sixty years later I would have a Thai grandson, I'd have been sure she was a phony. There he was, half a year old, on my lap, shaking and bouncing to Bob Marley. Austin loves to be jiggled to music, but his favorite contact is wet raspberry kisses.

A plump baby Buddha, his lush tan skin folds over Sumo wrestler muscles, his head cleanly shaven. His mom, Narm, explained it was the Buddhist way: "The ends of the hair are fire. Shaving them off keeps the baby cool."

Like most men I know, I don't relate well to infants until they can put two words together, play cars or army on the floor, or throw a ball. My children came later in life and they in turn had their own when they were older, but each has given me a grandson within the past two years. I thought I had fulfilled my need for a grandchild by having a third son at the age of fifty-eight, but now I'd been given two more boys, albeit at opposite ends of the earth.

Austin lives in the tropical paradise of Phuket, Thailand, giving me only a week to make a connection before my next visit would find him walking and talking. What is my reticence with infants about? I have a strong maternal drive for a man, but it's hard for me to relate to these little ones. Austin liked to be held facing outward so I couldn't feel his head snuggle against my chest, a skin-to-skin contact that could lead to instant feelings of love.

I found it easier to feel close to Austin in the warm, buoyant Andaman Sea where we played in the late afternoons. He splashed his arms up and down, squealing with laughter until the salt water stung his eyes. He seemed aching to swim or even surf like his dad Alex, or his young uncle Adam. Surfing with Alex this week gave Adam a brotherly closeness he's never had, despite their thirty-year age difference.

Austin has few toys, his play consisting mainly of being thrown in the air by Alex or held and fed by his mom. Bright colored lights and picture books also soothe him. Karen and I purchased a highchair for him, and to his parent's surprise he sat in it while we all ate together.

We also discovered a new game on the day we left.

Karen sang a song with lyrics I hadn't heard since Adam was a baby: "If you're happy and you know it, clap your hands … stomp your feet … shout hooray." Austin sat on my lap and we pranced to the music as we followed the actions of the song.

It had taken Bob Marley, raspberry kisses, swimming, bouncing, prancing, singing, dancing, smiles and hugs, but each day Austin and I fell in love a little more.

28

WHEN KAREN FELL OFF HER ASS ON HER ASS

Morocco, Christmas 2009

I HAD THOUGHT OF MOROCCO as a land of barren deserts and mysterious labyrinthine souks, a fusion of Arab, European, and African cultures. Adam was stoked about the exceptional waves breaking on its Atlantic Coast. Karen loved to photograph indigenous people, and I wanted to hike the High Atlas Mountains after learning that Scorsese substituted them for the Himalayas in *Kundun*, his film about the Dalai Lama. For me, Morocco was an opportunity to climb tall craggy peaks, and how many more could I do?

The hotel I chose, the Kasbah du Toubkal, was as romantic as its name, two story suites tumbling down a cliff in front of Massif Toubkal, the highest mountain in North

Africa at 13,676 feet.

After a hearty Moroccan breakfast of pancakes, jams, honey, and a cappuccino spiked with Starbucks instant, we began our hike. Two mules had been booked for us and we loaded them with water bottles and rain gear. Every few miles small villages cascaded down the cliffs, muddy brown concrete buildings like the pueblos of New Mexico but with cement water channels snaking between the homes.

The Berbers of Morocco are private people and resisted Karen's photography. Finally, two rouge-cheeked girls were ecstatic at getting ten dirhams each, about a buck and a quarter, and consented. If only we had more time to linger in the villages and get to know the people, but we were two hours behind after lunch and we needed to hustle to get back before dark.

Every mountain pass I struggled to climb offered panoramic vistas of snow-covered slopes, tempting Adam to want to ski them. After twelve mountainous miles my knees were aching in the same place they did when I ran my one and only marathon. I suggested we ride the mules for the last few miles.

Karen responded, "Why not? I'm ready for the fireplace at the Kasbah."

The donkey ride was so relaxing the pain slowly left my knees. Suddenly, a van careened around a curve, frightening her animal. The mule bucked in the air and headed down an embankment. Karen slid off, falling on her arm and backside just before the donkey jumped the creek, kicked its heels and fled.

More shaken than scratched, Karen realized she only had one shoe. We searched for fifteen minutes, but when the burro came into view, we saw her sneaker stuck precariously in the saddle. She mounted my donkey, flinching whenever a car passed or the riderless mule came close. The runaway's keeper finally grabbed its tail but let go when it dragged him toward a stone fence.

Just before nightfall, the guides trapped the burro in an alley and Karen recovered her shoe. We climbed our last hill surrounded by merchants hawking fossil geodes, silver bracelets, and coral necklaces. I turned to Karen, chuckled and said, "Tomorrow, let's do the camel trek!"

29

From Purgatory to Puya

Tana Toraja, Sulawesi, Indonesia—Summer 2010

I HAD NEVER SEEN a buffalo slaughtered nor a pig killed until I traveled to Toraja. Right before my eyes, dozens of pigs were butchered, squealing and squirming before hordes of onlookers after being skewered in the heart with a machete. But this barely prepared me for what followed; the ritual sacrifice of a buffalo.

The huge animal was tied to a stake in the center of a muddy field surrounded by hundreds of mourners and a few tourists. A fierce but determined man wearing a red headscarf, wagging a cigarette in one hand and holding a glistening machete in the other, stalked the huge animal. He hacked into its neck and with one blow severed the head, leaving a beating heart exposed just below the wound.

Sixteen-year-old Adam moved up to a spot just in front of the carnage and filmed the throbbing organ; his usually steady hands trembled when he lowered his camera. A bamboo chute carried blood from the buffalo's neck to the earth, freeing the spirit of the deceased elder of the household to ascend to heaven-like *puya* after a year in a purgatory-nowhere state. During this time the embalmed body would be kept in a special room of the family home.

Toraja is famous for its funeral celebrations, and I came to this isolated area of Indonesia in order to participate in one. Not only am I interested in tribal rituals, but also as I age I am drawn to how different cultures deal with death. I was prepared for the morbidity of the festivities by several days of celebrations, including a house blessing in which dozens of pigs were killed. The funeral rites continued for a week after we left and included the slaying of seven more buffalo. Long ago, human slaves or prisoners were sacrificed to enhance transcendence to *puya*.

The coffin containing the body of the elder, wrapped in bright red and yellow cloth with gold star-shaped sequins, was lifted high and borne out by ten men probably intoxicated on palm wine. They made their way across the muddy field, bouncing the coffin upwards towards *puya* while laughing and shouting to scare away bad spirits.

A daughter of the deceased, clothed in an elegant black dress, invited Karen, Adam, and I for lunch. Pork cooked in bamboo for Adam and vegetables and rice for us.

Next to the pavilion where we ate lunch was a dead pig, lying in a mixture of mud, feces, and blood. We had given the mourner's family a carton of cigarettes, a gift our guide had suggested. Karen was so taken by their graciousness that she crossed her hands over her heart, removed her earrings and gave them to our hostess.

The following day we visited a baby grave tree in which over thirty babies were buried. They were wrapped in cloth and placed in a carved hole in the tree, closed by a door of palm leaves. The tree eventually absorbs the body and carries its spirit skyward. Mothers mourning their children may support each other beside the complex roots of these magnificent Banyan trees and watch their children return to nature. To me, there is nothing as painful in life as the death of one's own child. How comforting it would be if I could believe Mother Nature brings the lost baby to heaven.

Near the baby graves are *tau-taus*, elegant effigies of wealthy deceased persons, placed in caves on the side of a mountain. They are carved from jackfruit wood that uncannily resembles human flesh. Their arms stretch forward with palms up as if to say "Join me. Do not be afraid."

Strewn near the caves are coffins collapsing from age, their contents of long bones and skulls spilling to the earth. Intrepid Adam posed by the skulls, asking Karen to take pictures for his Facebook page.

I have seen many bones before, in the majesty of Lalibela, Ethiopia, and the grim anguish of Auschwitz. I have observed open-air cremations in Varanasi, India, but never felt so welcomed to an endless pageant of the celebration of death.

Once again I was brought in touch with the inevitability of an ending to life, as I know it. What would it take to free my spirit to a peaceful, hovering state, I wondered. I was filled by the awe-inspiring mystery of it all.

30

BURNING MAN

Irvine, California, 2008

Karen dropped me off at an Outpatient Surgery Center in Irvine. A swarthy anesthesiologist asked me a few questions about my medical history then stuck a needle in my vein, quickly filling my brain with soothing Propofol, still commonly used for anesthesia despite having led to Michael Jackson's death.

My UCLA-trained eye surgeon had seemed competent when he operated on me a few years earlier, so I anticipated a quick, successful procedure. I lay on my back in the blissful nothingness of my drug-induced state. Suddenly I was jolted into consciousness. I sprang upright. A red ball of fire smashed into my face followed by the sickening odor of burning flesh.

I screamed, "I'm on fire!"

The surgeon shouted, "Water!" He dumped a metal basin full of cool liquid on my head. The fire went out, but the smell of burnt hair lingered as it did in an Indonesian funeral ceremony when the hair of squealing live pigs was torched off before roasting.

I fell back into my anesthetized sleep only to awaken to throbbing pain in the recovery room. My physician appeared troubled but tried to reassure me. "Basically, you got a free chemical peel of the top layer of your skin, maybe a little deeper in some places," he said. "You'd better see a burn specialist by tomorrow morning."

After asking for a mirror, I slowly raised it to the level of my chin. My face was red and raw, black and blue, swollen and misshapen. I looked like the victim of a heavyweight fight. My eyebrows and eyelashes were gone. Blisters of fluid would require the skillful hands of a plastic surgeon.

The doctor called Karen to come and take me home, telling her "We had a minor complication. There was a fire. It was immediately extinguished. It mainly affected the external layers of the skin of his face."

Karen entered the recovery room frightened, not knowing what to expect. She took one look, balled her fists and wailed, "He's deformed! What have you done to him? He was fine when I left him here."

Once home, I leaned on Karen as she helped me

to our bedroom, where I prepared myself for a few days of barely moving. Adam came downstairs to see me. He grabbed his camera, took pictures from every angle and at thirteen proclaimed "Dad, we're suing."

Later I learned that electro-cautery was used inches away from an oxygen mask, a dangerous and often prohibited combination. Adam was right!

Years afterward, I continue to look in the mirror and see my face as it was then, marred and grotesque. I have stopped dreaming of that ball of fire coming down on my face. When I light my gas fireplace on a windy day, the tips of flames leap out at me and barely singe the hairs of my skin. Once again I smell the swine of Sulawesi made ready for slaughter.

31

Fiftieth Medical School Reunion

Philadelphia, October 2010

I SKIPPED THE FIRST FORTY-NINE, but there was no way I was going to miss my fiftieth medical school reunion. I found my fellow members of the class of 1960 among the other sixty classes by squinting at the graduation pictures on their name badges. Each time I bent down to take in a boyish face, framed by a crew cut, I was flooded by a surge of memories.

One of the first to greet me was Harvey L., whom I'd known since high school. I was pleasantly surprised when I recalled he had played second base on our softball team and was part of a club I had wanted to join. They finally invited me when we were in twelfth grade but my mother said, "No, we can't afford to buy the zippered wool jacket." So I never became an official member of this cool group, every one of whom became a medical professional. But Harvey and I quickly made up for lost time, joking like we were fifteen again, making fun of all the *alter kockers* as if he and I were not also crotchety, fussy old men.

There were five Jewish doctors among the twenty-five attendees from my class. We huddled together at the party as we had at school, in part because Jefferson Medical College had a ten-percent Jewish quota back then. Another sign of the times was that Jeff didn't admit its first woman med student until the year after we graduated. Today, the majority of the medical students are women.

Why were over one hundred thirty-five of my fellow graduates not in attendance? Mike R. whispered the names of a handful that he knew had died. Some of the missing ones were among those I had longed to see the most. We had shared dissecting a cadaver, dating the same women, defending each other in near fistfights, and inhaling beer by the pitcher. I wondered who else among those absent had passed away? Had some felt too drained of brotherly love by our demanding education to return?

I recognized Bill H. by his still inquisitive bug-eyes. He was eighty now, having entered Jeff after serving in the Korean War. Bill tearfully said he had lost two wives and was dating again.

"They tell me I'm a good kisser," he said, his eyes widening even further and lighting up like a child's. Bill burst into song when he discovered he and Harvey had attended the same junior high. His sweet tenor voice brought back every word of the school anthem.

Len V.'s wife turned toward me and exclaimed, "Eddie Kaufman! You were the best dancer in the class." I couldn't possibly be given a greater compliment.

Often when a man in his seventies shares his deepest thoughts and feelings with me, he says something like, "You know, underneath this sagging skin, I'm still a teen-ager at heart." Dancing is one of the things I still do to feel young so I echoed her compliment. "Yeah, and I still dance to rock and roll at a bar called The Dirty Bird."

Each member of my class gave a brief summary of what they'd accomplished since graduation. Connie T. leaned on his cane and started the ceremonies. His wife told me he was battling recurrent prostate cancer. When he gave his talk he reminded me of Lou Gehrig's last speech at Yankee Stadium. Connie spoke of how lucky he was to have lived his life as a physician, husband, and father. Many of the men were quite proud of their grown children who were physicians and no one would admit to a son or daughter who had graduated from a medical school other than Jeff.

Bill sang another song after he shared his pleasure at having helped so many patients get sober. This time the lyrics of "Friends" reverberated throughout the room. I spoke briefly about what I'd done these many years. I wanted to pump my fist up and down and shout, "We did it! We've been doctors for fifty years!" I held back a bit and didn't raise my arm, but my voice quivered with pride. A photo of each member of our class was projected on a large screen. We all cheered when each one of the twenty-five of us were depicted.

I felt a strange love, affection, and kinship with this group of men I hadn't seen in half a century. Sure, I was the only one who didn't eat filet mignon or Philly cheese steak or who had a child under twenty, but I was one of them again. I wished we could put on our white coats and stethoscopes and march through the halls of the hospital together.

32

An Independent Surfer

Laguna Beach, Summer 2010

I REALIZED MY SON Adam was a fish from the moment his feet first hit the ocean. He picked up his brother's twenty-year-old soggy boogie-board and by six he rode the white water and at eight, the tube.

He surfed at nine, a long soft board on the gentle break of Doheny's beginner waves. Even then he showed balance and grace, crisscrossing his legs back and forth on his red board.

Adam and I watched a group of his sixth grade friends take a daily surf lesson at the Walk-on-Water Surf School. I encouraged him to join the group; Christian or not, they were the best in town.

"They're a bunch of kooks, Dad," he challenged, but

he paddled out and stayed with the group for three years till they became the nucleus of the Laguna Beach high school surf team.

In his first years of surfing Adam begged Karen and me to watch his every move. He would signal us and wait for our recognition, appreciation, and salutation before attempting his next wave.

He struggled at first in competitions, but in seventh grade he challenged Shorecliffs, the highest rated team in the country. The announcer named the final standings in reverse order. Two through six were called out and Adam's name was not among them. His dimpled face glowed with a look of acceptance-at-last. He had won his first surf meet!

At sixteen, Adam glides out to a head-high wave, quickly turns his board to shore, and with two rapid strokes maneuvers into the crashing water. He dips down to the base of the wave, flips back up to the top, rides along the crest and pumps down again. He repeats this movement several times, continuing to gain speed till he crouches into the curl. Frothy foam hides him until he emerges, standing gracefully, his arms extended, poised and ready to pounce.

"Wow!" I scream to Adam even before his feet hit the sand. "That was at least a nine. How did it feel to you?"

"It was a wave," he mutters.

"But what about the floater, the cuts and the barrel?" I try again to elicit a response.

An Independent Surfer

"Eddie, you don't even know what those words mean." He turns and quickly paddles out.

Adam has been calling me Eddie for years, and as disrespectful as it sounds I've grown used to it. I often find it affectionate. I can even handle his deprecating my use of surfing terminology. What really makes me furious is his lack of sharing his thoughts, feelings, and experiences with me. As a psychiatrist I know this is part of his adolescent individuation, but damn it, it hurts me.

When I watch him surf now, he does not wave or look for me. It is difficult to distinguish him from the others, often only silhouettes with the sun behind them. I shade my eyes and search for a signal that will help me spot him. No arm is raised. He won't let me see him. When will I see him and when will he see me again?

33

Ed's Epiphany

Everywhere, 2003-2010

I HAVE WATCHED KAREN MASTER fears of dirt, snorkeling and mice, and move on to embrace primitive villages, deep free-diving, and staring hyenas in the face. I have witnessed Adam surf the best waves in the world, climb the Himalaya, Patagonia and High Atlas Mountains, and perform for and play with children all over the earth. Karen has become an accomplished photographer and Adam a budding cinematographer, Karen a Buddhist practitioner and Adam a defiant adolescent.

But what have I accomplished as a result of a lifetime of travel, particularly the last seven years with Karen and Adam? Well, I have become a better writer. You have no idea how badly I wrote when I began my MFA program, or perhaps you do from the quality of my first few travel stories; however, I have rewritten them dozens of times, so you may not be able to tell the difference between earlier and later.

Travel taught me to observe by slowing down, lingering, looking, and having no expectations about outcome. By experiencing the world at a slower pace and paying attention to what I see, smell, hear, taste, and touch, I not only improve my writing but deepen my appreciation of existence. Writing from different viewpoints helps me understand more fully my multiple roles in life, not only as author, narrator, and character, but also as husband, divorcee, father, son, grandfather, and grandson.

I have learned to understand the biases I bring to my observations, to take more responsibility for how I see others and for my share of differences and disagreements and provocation of others. My first feedback from mentors and fellow students was personally devastating, but I have learned to regard critiques and particularly careful, detailed ones as loving acts that help me deepen my writing.

It is still difficult to let go of an investment in my words and eliminate sentences, passages, pages or an entire story. The realization that words are over-idealized extensions of myself helps me relinquish my most precious phrases.

Perhaps my most delightful surprise has been in the area of memory. I am amazed how quickly vivid memories and long forgotten emotions return when my aging forgetful mind delves into the past to write a memoir. Not only do feelings of guilt and yearning come back but also visions of worn furniture and musty smells of home. Continuing to use my brain in this way should help stave off the inevitable decline in memory that takes place with aging.

It will always be a struggle to tell a story that may hurt family and friends. My parents' deaths make it easier to write about them. But critical and accepting parents live on inside all of us. Their inner voices tell us not to write about them, break their rules, or tell their secrets. Recognition of these sources of my inhibitions has freed me to travel almost anywhere as well as write more spontaneously about my most painful issues.

Creative writing helps me view myself more objectively and substitute spontaneous thoughts for sequential ones, a very freeing process; one that Freud once said was the aim of psychoanalysis. When I write knowledgeably, I can separate from guilt, self-pity, revenge, anger, and even love. I cannot write about feelings or events until I have achieved a certain level of emotional distance from them. Yet in writing we can gain deep understanding. My goal when I began to write was art and not insight, but I have learned that the two are inseparable.

I have certainly filled my bottomless bucket list and learned a lot about aging, dying, and an empty nest that never seems to come. Each of my journeys enriched me during months of planning, enthralled me during my adventure, and provided years of memories. Traveling and writing brought more insights about myself than my five years of training psychoanalysis.

Pilgrimages to places like Varanasi, Lalibela, and Tibetan monasteries have helped me accept my powerlessness over the inevitability of my death. But slowly and surely they have convinced me of the existence of one god, whatever his or her name may be. This belief has helped me to accept all religions and to pray in all sacred buildings, no matter the name of the church or temple. Yet you may ask, "Where's the epiphany? Where's the answer for Ed about the mystery of a soul, of an afterlife? At the age of seventy-five I'm still searching for answers to these questions. Perhaps I should go back to Tibet and debate these issues among the monks with a loud clap of my hands. For now I'll just keep traveling and learning, a little at a time.

Acknowledgements

I AM EXCEEDINGLY GRATEFUL to everyone who shepherded me through the process of transition from an author of psychiatric texts to a creative writer. Since I still have a linear mind, I will list them chronologically. Julie Brickman is not only the author of my introduction, but the first to suggest I embark on my new writing career by obtaining an MFA. Julie has continued to guide and mentor me throughout my struggles and the poetry of her own prose is an inspiration to me.

I owe a great debt to the faculty and students at Antioch University, Los Angeles who touched and supported me. Special thanks to Eloise Klein-Healy, founder, and Steve Heller, director of the program, and my first mentors Brenda Miller and David Ulin for the gentle confrontation I desperately needed my first year. Also to Valerie Boyd, who sensitized me to race and culture, and Sharman Apt Russell who helped me to follow my bliss.

Several extended workshops have been very helpful, particularly Rose-Ellen Brown in Spoleto, Italy, and Kaylie Jones at the Norman Mailer Writers Colony in Provincetown, Mass. Another continuing invaluable resource is Dime Stories, an organization that sponsors three-minute readings that tell a complete story. This venue has taught me to condense my work to bare truths and eliminate a lot of unnecessary material. Meredith Resnick, founder of Orange County Dime Stories, and current leader Michelle McCormick have both aided me in this process. I am also grateful to Chris Weaver of Laguna Beach Books for his advice and encouragement during the early phase of shaping the manuscript of *From Monks to Mountain Gorillas*.

I had never heard of writing-critique groups until several years ago, but I have found one to be quite worthwhile. This group, superbly led by Janet Simcic, has been more helpful than I could ever have imagined, especially Dennis J. Phinney, the master of active verbs; Ana Arellano, the voice of youth; Brenda Barrie, ethnic expert; John Gray, for his lyrical essay skills; and Ron Hoefer, prodder.

My family adventures would have been lonely solo journeys without Karen and Adam, who let me drag them all over the world to places we'd never heard of before. I admire Karen so much for her growth as a meditator, photographer, snorkeler, hiker, and donkey rider, and her unique ability to touch and be touched by people all over the world. I am grateful to Adam for the many ways he comes through when it appears he won't.

Lastly, an encomium of orchids to Allene Symons, who is not only my editor and publisher, but also a true friend in every way the word friend is used.

LOCATIONS FOR EACH CHAPTER

1. Philadelphia, Pa.
2. Grand Canyon, Ariz.
3. Shelter Island, N.Y.
4. Laguna Beach, Calif.
5. Tanzania
6. Botswana, Zimbabwe
7. Laguna Beach, Calif.
8. Philadelphia
9. Bangkok, Thailand
10. Phuket, Thailand
11. Costa Rica
12. Tibet
13. Tibet
14. Kodiak Island, Alaska
15. Sayulita, Mexico
16. Philadelphia
17. Galapagos Islands
18. Galapagos Islands
19. Catalina Island, Calif.
20. Namibia
21. Papua New Guinea
22. Varanasi, India
23. Southern Ethiopia
24. Rwanda
25. Northern Ethiopia
26. Brooklyn, N.Y.
27. Phuket, Thailand
28. Morocco
29. Sulawesi, Indonesia
30. Irvine, Calif.
31. Philadelphia
32. California Beaches
33. The World

www.ingramcontent.com/pod-product-compliance
Lightning Source LLC
Chambersburg PA
CBHW031242290426
44109CB00012B/406